Crossword

POWERED BY Cats and Coffee

Puzzles

Designer Ink.

- REVIEWS -

YOUR THOUGHTS AND REVIEWS ARE ALWAYS APPRECIATED ON AMAZON, JUST - ONE OR TWO LINES IS HELPFUL

THANK YOU - ENJOY THE BOOK!

Solutions

Page 104

Across

1. State in NE India
6. Support, in a way
10. Animal trainer tool
14. A system of solmization
15. Limitless quantities
16. Hokkaido people
17. Cartoon canine
18. Prompt willingness
20. An acrobatic feat
22. Nautical pole
23. Clairvoyance, e.g.
24. Breathalyzer attachment
27. Autocrats of old
30. 58-40 million years ago. Presence of modern mammals
32. Greenish blue
35. Cross
37. Claw
38. Women in habits
39. Holdover
41. A rapid series of short loud sounds
42. A person's manner of walking
44. Obi, e.g.
45. Tournament passes
46. Favor
48. Safari sight
50. Get prone
51. Essence
53. Physics lab device, for short
56. Easy to use
60. Don't pay retail
63. Tiny part
64. Sign of boredom
65. Willingly
66. Enlighten
67. It towers over Taormina
68. Middle of March
69. Begin

Down

1. Egyptian snakes
2. Flies alone
3. Failure
4. Taste lingers
5. Relatives of Tahitians
6. Cruising
7. Swain
8. Top scout
9. African fly
10. Potter's tool
11. Get going
12. Connections
13. Inflammation
19. Move, as a plant
21. First Super Bowl M.V.P.
24. Fasten a boat to a bitt, pin, or cleat
25. Lizards that can change skin colour
26. Pool contents?
28. Some deer
29. Kind of battery
31. Stew of onions and beer
32. A rival
33. Somewhat
34. Come together
36. Gossip, slangily
40. Some like it hot
43. Brains
47. Breakfast cereal
49. Clan members
52. Pigtail, e.g.
54. Acknowledge
55. Chin indentation
56. Arm part
57. Beat it
58. Judges
59. It's used to walk the dog
60. The 25th letter of the Roman alphabet
61. Pillbox, e.g.
62. Fess (up)

PUZZLE 1

1	2	3	4	5		6	7	8	9		10	11	12	13
14						15					16			
17						18			19					
20				21										
	22						23				24	25	26	
		27		28	29		30		31				
32	33	34		35		36		37					
38				39			40		41				
42			43		44				45				
46				47		48		49					
50				51		52		53			54	55	
		56				57	58						59
60	61	62							63				
64					65				66				
67					68				69				

Across

1. High in the Andes
5. Audition
9. Happening place
14. Missle
15. Freudian topics
16. Spy, at times
17. Failure to keep a promise (of marriage)
20. Symbol of might
21. Diva's delivery
22. Construct
23. Healthful retreats
24. Maple genus
25. Debtor's accounts of money he owes;
32. ___ Ste. Marie
33. Nile reptiles
34. Rural sight
35. Snowman prop
36. Bar stock
37. Parts of a code
38. Hot blood
39. Protection
41. Home with a view
42. Devoid of passion or feeling
46. Aid and ___
47. Seat of Garfield County, Okla.
48. Busybody
50. Shot, e.g.
51. Kind of approval
54. Question phrased in such a way as to suggest the desired answer;
57. Alleviated
58. Willa Cather's "One of ___ "
59. Golden rule word
60. "So ___!"
61. Pizazz
62. "___ here long?"

Down

1. Early pulpit
2. Money in the banca
3. Arduous journey
4. Reproductive cells
5. 1943 conference site
6. Altruist's opposite
7. Crash site?
8. Sugar amt.
9. How many ____ in that buildings?
10. Captures time
11. Huge
12. Birth place
13. Before, to Burns
18. A headlike protuberance on an organ or structure
19. Go over
23. It's under a foot
24. Church alcove
25. Savory jelly
26. Arab capital
27. A small porous bowl made of bone ash
28. Authority
29. Roar
30. Carl the sprinter
31. Lets up
36. Brawl
37. Do banker's work
39. State of decline
40. Collect slowly
41. "I'm outta here!"
43. Small scales from animal skins
44. Take exception to
45. Catch
48. "Awright!"
49. Dexterity
50. Greenish-blue
51. D.C. al ___ (musical direction)
52. Spoil, with "on"
53. Auth. unknown
54. Book end?
55. Word on all U.S. coins
56. It has a certain ring to it

PUZZLE 2

Across

1. A medieval musical instrument resembling a trombone
8. Valuable goods
13. Disorganized
14. At the same time that
16. Nearly, but not exactly, conical
17. Open to or abounding in fresh air
18. Water carrier
19. Tests by lifting
21. Attempt
22. Founded: Abbr.
25. Bundle
27. Petting zoo animal
30. "Come again?"
31. Durable wood
34. Morse bit
35. Table part
37. Exclamation of frustration, rage, shock, etc.
38. Japanese sash
39. An unnaturally frenzied or distraught woman
41. Elbow's site
42. A small vascular growth
44. Get ready to drive
45. Driving need
46. Peter, Paul and Mary, e.g.
47. "I can't believe it!"
48. Specialty
50. It's a numbers game
52. Friend in the 'hood
53. Commonly
55. Swelling
57. Bookie's quote
61. Sad
63. Exhausted as a result of longtime stress
66. Oil
67. The cause of a disease
68. Long
69. Cops and _____

Down

1. Falling flakes
2. Stridex target
3. Spasmodic movements of the body and limbs
4. A colourful ornamental carp
5. Evil
6. 2002 Winter Olympics locale
7. Your digits
8. Watch brand
9. Beat or _____ the eggs
10. Lungful
11. Beautiful people
12. Palm reader, e.g.
13. Chill
15. Like some humor
20. All the animal life in a particular region or period
23. Little rascal
24. Spanish appetizer
26. Capt.'s guess
27. Embrace
28. Done for wage
29. A person who is uninterested in intellectual pursuits
32. Be in harmony
33. A native or inhabitant of Cambodia
36. Second shot
37. In accordance with
40. Asinine
43. "Yeah, ___!"
47. Part of MOMA
49. Flute sound
51. Block
53. Giant Giant
54. Donnybrook
56. Camera setting
58. It's in a jamb
59. An udder, breast or teat
60. It's often sloppy
62. Cousin of calypso
64. Kid
65. Head, slangily

PUZZLE 3

Across

1. Mary in the White House
5. Disorder
10. Contributes
14. Fluish feeling
15. Kind of group, in chemistry
16. Carrot, e.g.
17. Beauties
18. A female actor in a comedy
20. Ritual samurai suicide
22. Cow
23. Dentist's directive
24. A hill or ridge with one face steep and the opposite face gently sloping
26. A change for the worse
30. Unfasten the pins of
31. Open, as an envelope
32. Dope
35. Auricular
36. Comics sound
38. Dog command
39. Cold porter fan?
40. Expunge
41. A red fluorescent dye (Cosmetics)
42. Worn by exposure to the weather
45. Look down on with disdain
49. Holiday ___
50. Cognizant
51. Small swift graceful antelope
55. A disposition to laugh
58. Letter after theta
59. Pest
60. Emergency supply
61. Decant
62. Gawk at
63. Bullwinkle, e.g.
64. ___ row

Down

1. Makes it
2. S-shaped molding
3. Eyesore
4. Characteristic of an absolute ruler
5. Gets in with a computer
6. Measure
7. A healthy capacity for vigorous activity
8. Four quarters
9. Atlantic food fish
10. Blocks
11. Coffee break snack
12. Ritchie Valens hit on the flip side of "La Bamba"
13. Cancel, as of a correction or deletion
19. Clarification lead-in
21. At the time of
24. RC, e.g.
25. Building block
26. Couples
27. Fascinated by
28. Fast-moving card game
29. Cay
32. Comme ci, comme ca
33. Mideast chief: Var.
34. Ivy League team
36. Come across as
37. Arrange
38. Yellow flowered swamp plant
40. Dork
41. Sea flier
43. Break
44. Pepsin, e.g.
45. Boatload
46. Because of, with "to"
47. Kind of spray
48. Hackneyed
51. Copter's forerunner
52. Peer
53. Decorative case
54. Reddish-brown gem
56. School of thought
57. ___ Getz ("Lethal Weapon 2" role for Joe Pesci)

PUZZLE 4

1	2	3	4		5	6	7	8	9		10	11	12	13
14					15						16			
17					18					19				
20				21						22				
		23					24	25						
26	27	28				29								
30						31						32	33	34
35					36	37				38				
39				40					41					
			42			43	44							
45	46	47	48			49								
50					51						52	53	54	
55				56	57					58				
59				60					61					
62				63					64					

Across

1. Bucket of bolts
5. Smelting waste
9. Bring down
14. Early pulpit
15. Bubbly drink
16. A small wooded area
17. Loving 2 countries
20. Barfly's binge
21. Bartlett's abbr.
22. A robber
25. And tribulations
29. Ancient Greek theatre
30. Many a dictator's problem
32. Somewhat, in music
33. Fate
34. Peculiar
35. Hard to pin down or identify
39. Something to believe in
41. Some kind of a nut
42. Dec. holiday
45. Can't speak, can't hear
47. Unite
49. Bow
50. Streaked
51. Used as fertilizer
53. Baby holder
54. Several plants of the family Onagraceae
61. Eats no animal or dairy
62. Diva's solo
63. Midmonth date
64. Spurred
65. Catch, in a way
66. Rectangular paving stone

Down

1. Conned
2. Cousin of an ostrich
3. Legal org.
4. Characterized by complete cowardliness
5. A descendant or heir
6. Soprano Lehmann
7. Clay, now
8. ___ Strip
9. Eccentric
10. _____ and Herzegovina
11. Cigarette's end
12. Go downhill fast?
13. Sixth sense, for short
18. Masked critter
19. Put away, in a way
22. Cut
23. Flurry
24. Point
26. Absence of the sense of smell
27. Jack-in-the-box part
28. Blue
30. A high wave caused by tidal flow
31. Beam
33. Bow
36. Large tropical seed pod with very tangy pulp
37. Insight
38. A label identifying the owner of a book in which it is pasted
39. Driver's lic. and others
40. Main
43. Deed
44. "What did I tell you?"
46. All the animal life in a particular region or period
47. A stripe or stripes of contrasting colour
48. Governessy
50. Money substitute
52. Lab gel
54. Cain raiser
55. Engage in passive relaxation
56. Salad ingredient
57. For
58. Horatian work
59. Firm
60. French 101 verb

PUZZLE 5

1	2	3	4		5	6	7	8		9	10	11	12	13
14					15					16				
17				18					19					
			20					21						
22	23	24						25				26	27	28
29							30	31						
32					33						34			
		35		36	37					38				
39	40			41							42		43	44
45			46					47	48					
49							50							
			51		52		53							
54	55	56				57					58	59	60	
61					62					63				
64					65					66				

Across

1. "___ the night before..."
5. Fell off
10. Mucus
14. Full-bodied
15. God
16. Artifice
17. Shore soarer
18. Arm bones
19. ___ of Wight
20. Ship part
21. Bill's partner
22. "Super!"
23. A varnish for wood consisting of shellac dissolved in alcohol
27. Physicist who proposed the exclusion principle
30. Security
31. Constellation between Great Bear and Orion
33. Golf ball position
34. Bar selections
38. London square
41. Fit as a fiddle
42. Craggy peak
43. Peak
44. Trim
46. Church recesses
47. Half-free from work day
52. Accustom
53. Actor Alastair
54. Pack (down)
58. Japanese stringed instrument
59. Money for silence
61. Organic compound
62. Fall locale
63. Lizards that can change skin colour
64. First-class
65. Breather
66. More rational
67. Door opener

Down

1. Hike
2. Kind of service
3. Teen affliction
4. How long does it last?
5. Bring out
6. Be owned by; be in the possession of
7. Vision involving the use of both eyes
8. Capt.'s prediction
9. Batiking need
10. Flow in a circular current, of liquids
11. Japanese-American
12. Leaf strip used for writing
13. Choppers
22. Pan, e.g.
24. Baltic port
25. "Aquarius" musical
26. Iron
27. Approach
28. Ambience
29. Caspian Sea feeder
32. E'en if
34. Steak cut from the back side
35. Thanksgiving dish
36. Lackawanna's lake
37. Fixes
39. Good shot
40. Dock
44. Any boat
45. Like some mushrooms
47. Mountain exerciser
48. + end
49. Plucked instrument having a pear-shaped body
50. Attack locale
51. An independent ruler or chieftain
55. Before long
56. Pre-stereo
57. Commoner
59. ___-Rhin (Strasbourg's department)
60. Genetic initials

PUZZLE 6

1	2	3	4		5	6	7	8	9		10	11	12	13
14					15						16			
17					18						19			
20					21					22				
			23	24				25	26					
27	28	29				30								
31				32		33				34	35	36	37	
38					39			40						
41				42			43							
		44				45		46						
47	48	49	50				51							
52					53				54	55	56	57		
58				59	60				61					
62				63					64					
65				66					67					

15

Across

1. After
5. Checks
9. Kind of concerto
14. Away from the wind
15. Gumbo vegetable
16. Screen letters
17. Scruff
18. Omani money
19. Nocturnal badger-like carnivore
20. A song celebrating the joys of drinking
23. Cremona craftsman
24. Helped
28. Baseball datum
32. ___-Lorraine
33. Disposed to pray or appearing to pray
37. Stubborn beast
38. A billion years
39. Compel by coercion, threats, or crude means
42. Pinup's leg
43. Dedicated
45. Stop
47. Prompt
50. Exodus commemoration
51. A logging sled
53. Horse pull
57. A very small town with few facilities
61. Slip
64. Small buffalo of the Celebes
65. Creative spark
66. ___ Kane of "All My Children"
67. Archeological site
68. Foreboding
69. Key
70. Archipelago part
71. Coupling

Down

1. ___ bear
2. Eye opener
3. Certain print
4. Wee
5. Actress Spelling
6. Cognate
7. Act the blowhard
8. Hot stuff
9. Springy?
10. Used common speech in free verse with clear concrete imagery
11. Cereal grain
12. Golfer's concern
13. ___ right
21. Increase the amount (of a check) fraudulently
22. Seeds
25. Expression of joy
26. Bravura
27. Considers
29. Flub
30. At a distance
31. A racing sled for one or two people
33. Active; lively; brisk
34. Vagabond
35. Soul
36. Miner's quest
40. Antiquated
41. Heiress, perhaps
44. Break
46. Make happy or satisfied
48. Like some yogurt
49. Game piece
52. Lewis with Lamb Chop
54. Isuzu model
55. Fine-tune
56. Animal catcher
58. Burden
59. Irritate
60. Balanced
61. Many Chinese dynasty
62. Store posting: Abbr.
63. Bother

PUZZLE 7

1	2	3	4		5	6	7	8		9	10	11	12	13
14					15					16				
17					18					19				
20				21				22						
23							24				25	26	27
		28		29	30	31		32					
33	34	35					36			37			
38				39				40	41		42		
43			44		45					46			
47			48	49		50							
51					52			53		54	55	56
		57				58	59	60					
61	62	63				64				65			
66					67				68				
69					70				71				

Across

1. Maid's cloth
4. Chows down
8. ___ apso (dog)
13. Crackerjack
14. Aweather's opposite
15. Corrupt
16. Everyone votes
19. The hulled and crushed grain of various cereals
20. Legal prefix
21. Baptist leader?
22. Discompose
23. Mouth-like opening in a sponge through which water is expelled
25. Nicholas II was the last one
27. Obviously surprised
31. "The ___ Daba Honeymoon"
34. Hightailed it
36. Bewitch
37. Morning criers
40. Pride and prejudice, for example
41. Codger
42. Any ship
43. Restrict
44. Goes down
46. Abandon
50. A voluptuously beautiful young woman
54. Geologic time period
57. Amble
58. Check payee, maybe
59. A swindle in which you cheat at gambling
62. Focal point
63. Donut-shaped surfaces
64. Dug in
65. By way of
66. Lip-___
67. Mason's burden

Down

1. Reggae that incorporates hip hop, rhythm and blues and sampling
2. Biting

3. Andrea Doria's domain
4. Momentous
5. "C'est la vie"
6. Abbr. to the left of a number
7. Oozes
8. Numbs a particular area of the body
9. Big success
10. Flu source
11. Any day now
12. "The King and I" role
15. Big copper exporter
17. Bridge position
18. Fond du ___, Wis.
23. Certain cookie
24. "Holy mackerel!"
26. Pitches in
28. Old Testament book
29. "'Tain't nothin'!"
30. Gaelic language
31. Does something
32. Imperfectly crystallized or coarse diamonds,
33. Small dark purple fruit
35. Sawbones
36. "What ___?"
38. Giving
39. Fine powdery material
45. Go parasailing
47. Fountain order
48. Christmas ___
49. Doesn't own
51. Dickens's ___ Heep
52. Odd-numbered page
53. Angry
54. Almond
55. Some deer
56. Debate side
58. European capital
60. Half a sawbuck
61. Not forthright

PUZZLE 8

Across

1. ___ President
6. Awry
11. Tennessee athlete, for short
14. Astound
15. Fixin' to
16. Bygone polit. cause
17. Receives radar signals
19. Cheat, slangily
20. A plant body without true stems
21. Now and then
23. Moray, e.g.
24. Dotty
25. Chesterfield, e.g.
28. Brinks
32. "Yadda, yadda, yadda"
33. Party time, maybe
34. Kind of jack
36. Court figures
39. Be a snitch
41. Big mess
42. ___ podrida
43. Digging, so to speak
44. Atlas, e.g.
45. "Fantasy Island" prop
46. Blouse, e.g.
48. A kind of computer architecture
49. Container for nitroglycerin
50. The arrangement of the hair
53. "Rocky ___"
55. Theoretically
57. An imaginary creature
61. Big, fat mouth
62. The lowest atmospheric layer
64. Pandowdy, e.g.
65. Construction girder
66. Tear open
67. Ashes holder
68. Dermatologist's concerns
69. Airs

Down

1. K follower
2. Asian nurse
3. Arp's art
4. Flowering shrub
5. Actress Oberon
6. Long, long time
7. Extinct flightless bird
8. Ancient Andean
9. Nasal mucus
10. The Siouan language
11. Pasta in strings thinner than spaghetti
12. Architectural projection
13. Run out, as a subscription
18. Tall marsh plant
22. Foreword, for short
25. Son of Ramses I
26. Baker
27. Trade name - Magic Marker
29. ___ tube
30. Algonquian tribe member
31. Chesterfields, e.g.
35. Diplomatic representative of the Pope
37. Dog biter
38. Attack, with "into"
40. Washing sponge
47. Relating to or promoting digestion
49. Hindu divinity
50. Aquatic South American rodent
51. Broadcasting
52. Churchill Downs event
54. Enter
56. Some deer
57. Soccer ___
58. Beach bird
59. Ashtabula's lake
60. Gym set
63. Congratulations, of a sort

PUZZLE 9

1	2	3	4	5		6	7	8	9	10		11	12	13
14						15						16		
17					18							19		
20							21			22				
		23					24							
25	26	27			28	29	30	31		32				
33				34				35		36		37	38
39			40		41					42			
43					44						45		
		46		47		48				49			
50	51				52				53	54			
55						56		57			58	59	60
61				62			63						
64				65					66				
67				68					69				

Across
1. Little bird
4. "Your turn"
8. "Check this out!"
12. Deep sleep
13. Delhi dress
14. Loose hemp
16. Final, e.g.
17. "Hogwash!"
18. Grassy plain
19. Napoleon, e.g.
20. Carbonium, e.g.
21. Coquettish
23. Bill
24. Glower
26. "Tarzan" extra
28. Aged
30. "Don't ___!"
32. Clarified butter used in Indian cookery
36. The property possessed by a large mass
39. Blue shade
41. Chaps
42. Back, in a way
43. Beside
45. Drink from a dish
46. The Kennedys, e.g.
48. Flexible mineral
49. "No problem!"
50. LP player
51. Hallucinogen
52. Chest protector
54. Floral necklace
56. Corpulent
60. "That's ___ ..."
63. "___ alive!"
65. Australian runner
67. Cambridge sch.
68. Brandish
70. "Comme ci, comme ça"
72. Barber's supply
73. Host
74. Go for
75. Punjabi believer
76. Bar order
77. Friends and neighbors
78. Carry on

Down
1. Harmful
2. Adult insect
3. Cap
4. Christiania, now
5. Conceited
6. "___ on my bed my limbs I lay": Coleridge
7. A kind of computer architecture
8. A small vascular growth
9. "Do the Right Thing" pizzeria owner
10. 32-card game
11. Charlie, for one
12. A large edible mushroom
15. Kind of rule
20. "___ say!"
22. Common deciduous tree
25. Moo goo gai pan pan
27. Baby carrier?
29. ___ lab
30. Bypass
31. In ___ (harmonious)
33. ___ Bowl
34. An unfledged or nestling hawk
35. Catch a glimpse of
36. "Goldberg Variations" composer
37. ___ fruit
38. Baker's unit
40. "___ for the poor"
44. Blah-blah-blah
47. Bubkes
49. "Chicago" lyricist
51. On, as a lamp
53. Chit
55. Downy duck
57. Internet messages
58. Having a smooth, gleaming surface
59. Carve in stone
60. "I ___ you one"
61. Darkens
62. Art ___
64. Hit
65. Atlantic Coast states, with "the"
66. Don't believe it
69. Money in Moldova
71. A colourful ornamental carp
72. Cooking meas.

PUZZLE 10

23

Across

1. U.S.S.R. successor
4. Fill-in
8. Gumbo
12. Bang-up
13. Between an axis and an offshoot
14. Meat from a calf
16. Cat's scratcher
17. Bridges of Los Angeles County
18. Baffled
19. Reddish brown
21. ___ of the Unknowns
23. Wild goose having white adult plumage
24. Artist's asset
25. Prepare to swallow
27. "___ Baby Baby" (Linda Ronstadt hit)
29. Ticket info, maybe
30. Chop (off)
31. Band booking
34. Humans, e.g.
37. Place to trade
38. Altar avowal
39. Clickable image
40. Chicken ___
41. Deuce topper
42. Born, in bios
43. Bounce back, in a way
45. Roaring sound
47. "Silent Spring" subject
48. Pan, e.g.
49. "Bye now"
50. Appear, with "up"
51. Sound of rapid vibration
52. ___ grecque (cooked in olive oil, lemon juice, wine, and herbs, and served cold)
55. Way, way off
58. Departure
60. The third axis in a 3-dimensional coordinate system
62. Prepare to surf, perhaps
64. Santa ___, Calif.
66. (maths) hyperbolic sine
67. "Fantastic!"
68. During
69. Shrewd
70. Think or believe
71. Cravings
72. 1969 Peace Prize grp.

Down

1. Of the cod family
2. Absurd
3. Iced, with "up"
4. Can opener
5. English cathedral city
6. Cat's cry
7. Pudding fruit
8. Eggs
9. A sailing vessel with two masts
10. Foolhardy
11. Safe, on board
12. Be sore
15. Gabriel, for one
20. Battery contents
22. Crude dude
26. "For ___ a jolly ..."
28. Decide to leave, with "out"
29. Big ___ Conference
30. Calif. airport
31. Copter's forerunner
32. Footnote word
33. A Christian as contrasted with a Jew
34. Fasten
35. Bumped off
36. Keats, for one
37. ___ juice (milk)
40. High degree
41. "___ bad!"
43. "I" problem
44. Endure
45. As follows
46. Tease
49. Drive in front of another vehicle
50. 2002 Olympics venue
51. Ecological community
52. Kind of skeleton
53. Fast talk
54. Far from ruddy
55. Priestly garb
56. Fortified military post
57. Biology lab supply
59. Inside shot?
61. Fungal spore sacs
63. "___ what?"
65. Infomercials, e.g.

PUZZLE 11

Across

1. Increase, with "up"
4. More, in Madrid
7. Sandler of "Big Daddy"
11. Jewish month
12. Charades, e.g.
13. "M*A*S*H" setting
15. A temporary resident
17. Accumulate
18. Blood letters
19. Various rich and elaborate cakes
21. "___, humbug!"
22. The "p" in m.p.g.
23. Pinocchio, at times
24. Delight
27. Flipper
28. An odd, fanciful or capricious idea
30. "How ___ Mehta Got Kissed, Got Wild, and Got a Life" (Kaavya Viswanathan novel in the news)
33. Part of BYO
36. Arouse
38. Conclusion
39. Schuss, e.g.
40. Deceive
41. Curacao neighbor
43. "___ go!"
45. Coral ___
46. The starting form of anything
48. Nod, maybe
50. Information unit
51. Building near a silo
53. Costa del ___
56. "___ any drop to drink": Coleridge
58. Magazine feature
60. Absorbed, as a loss
61. Clear, as a disk
64. (of aircraft) fit to fly
66. End of the quip
67. Detective, at times
68. Goes quickly
69. Bad look
70. "___ pales in Heaven the morning star": Lowell
71. "___ the fields we go"

Down

1. Building block
2. Blair's predecessor
3. Adept
4. Kind of ray
5. An independent ruler or chieftain
6. "Buona ___" (Italian greeting)
7. Alias preceder
8. State or condition
9. Dancer in a conventional pose
10. ___ Verde National Park
11. "By yesterday!"
12. Covered with particles resembling meal
14. ___ Wednesday
16. Wrinkly fruit
20. "Gross!"
25. Back talk
26. An American in Paris, maybe
27. Out of condition
28. Habeas corpus, e.g.
29. Christmas season
30. Mozart's "L'___ del Cairo"
31. Dermatologist's concern
32. Foreshadow
34. ___ Fjord
35. Arthur Godfrey played it
37. "Thank You (Falettinme Be Mice ___ Agin)" (#1 hit of 1970)
42. "A jealous mistress": Emerson
44. Poor handwriting
47. "Absolutely!"
49. Annul
51. Pipe material
52. Cliffside dwelling
53. "Socrate" composer
54. Additional
55. Grass uitable for grazing by livestock
56. "What's ___?"
57. Face-to-face exam
59. Cracker spread
62. "Comprende?"
63. "To ___ is human ..."
65. Frat letter

PUZZLE 12

Across

1. Small round bread
6. Final: Abbr.
9. Clarified butter used in Indian cookery
13. French romance
14. Born, in Bordeaux
15. Slender long-beaked fish
16. Bass member of the viol family
17. Flat hat
18. Like "The X-Files"
19. A government order imposing a trade barrier
21. Prayer book
23. Ballad
24. Contemptible one
25. "Is that ___?"
28. Elder, e.g.
30. Punctuation mark
35. Book part
37. Cantina cooker
39. Played by rubbing a stick or scraper
40. A lightweight hat worn
41. Gallery of art
43. Old Chinese money
44. About
46. Opening time, maybe
47. Strengthen, with "up"
48. Load anew
50. Call for
52. Large amount of money
53. Crosspiece
55. Directly
57. Aquatic animal forming mossy colonies
61. Polygonal base and triangular sides
65. W.W. II conference site
66. Also
68. Chip away at
69. Link
70. Blackguard
71. Attendance counter
72. "Desire Under the ___"
73. "48 ___"
74. Lug

Down

1. Beep
2. Mosque V.I.P.
3. Archaeological find
4. Of or relating to occurring in a tube
5. Ancient debarkation point
6. "Do ___ others as..."
7. Grassy area
8. Beat
9. Highlander
10. Disabled
11. Border lake
12. Appraiser
15. Gob
20. Greek sandwiches
22. Amniotic ___
24. An act of narration
25. Church part
26. Freetown currency unit
27. Mike holder
29. Dash
31. One of mixed breed
32. Cat's cry
33. Hippodrome, e.g.
34. Like a shoe
36. The driest variety of sherry
38. Blue-ribbon
42. Destitute
45. A man raised by apes
49. The Righteous Brothers, e.g.
51. Coercion
54. "But of course!"
56. Our "mother"
57. Memory unit
58. Commuting option
59. (cosmology) the original matter
60. "Miss ___ Regrets"
61. Miniature sci-fi vehicles
62. Churn
63. Doing nothing
64. Abstruse
67. Propel, in a way

PUZZLE 13

Across

1. People person
6. Hems' partners
10. Cut
14. Express
15. City on the Yamuna River
16. Quaker's "you"
17. Percolate
18. Place of worship for a Jewish congregation
19. Stick in one's ___
20. The earth
22. Retentive
24. "It's no ___!"
25. (cosmology) the original matter
27. Neat and smart in appearance
29. Jump across
33. Deviation
34. Door sign
35. Alliance
37. Devil
41. "Crikey!"
42. Needles
44. 16 1/2 feet
45. Alpha's opposite
48. Capital of ancient Chinese empire
49. ___ fruit
50. Abate
52. Treat badly
54. Directions for making something
58. Arizona city
59. Amber, e.g.
60. Farfetched
62. Bottle-shaped pins used in bowling
66. Bad day for Caesar
68. "O Sanctissima," e.g.
70. Beauty pageant wear
71. "Blue" or "White" river
72. Dynasty in which Confucianism and Taoism emerged
73. Dearie
74. Makeup, e.g.
75. Put up, as a picture
76. Correct, as text

Down

1. Stallion, once
2. Blunted blade
3. When repeated, a 1997 Jim Carrey comedy
4. Convert ordinary language into code
5. Interest
6. Consumes
7. Muslim honorific
8. A twisting squeeze
9. Pay
10. Abbr. after a comma
11. Make a rhythmic sound
12. "Cut it out!"
13. Carved
21. Novi Sad residents
23. Amount of work
26. Drops off
28. Be behind
29. Big name in construction
30. Midterm, e.g.
31. Assistant
32. Non-Jew
36. Allegation
38. Advocate
39. Pepsi, e.g.
40. Do some cutting, maybe
43. Atlas enlargement
46. Beauty
47. Adjoin
49. Used for nuclear fuels
51. Whiten
53. ___ fly
54. Pass out
55. Any Platters platter
56. Film units
57. ___ shirt (colorful garment)
61. Boxer Spinks
63. Leaf
64. Persia, now
65. An aromatic ointment used in antiquity
67. Undertake, with "out"
69. Big galoot

PUZZLE 14

Across

1. Indian bread
5. Comic Sandler
9. Clash
13. Inspired with confidence
16. Cork's country
17. A treatise on demons
18. "God's Little ___"
19. Proceeds
20. Percussion instrument
22. Voting "nay"
23. Losing proposition?
25. Farm cry
27. Lieu
30. "Get ___!"
32. Unagi, at a sushi bar
33. ___ brat
34. Bother
35. Constellation between Great Bear and Orion
38. Bird's beak
39. Peopled with settlers
41. Police, with "the"
42. Cold dessert
44. Durable wood
45. Hodgepodge
46. Blockhead
47. Chop off
48. Like some symmetry
49. Brunch cocktail
51. Fungal spore sacs
53. Fourposter, e.g.
54. Expert
56. A nest in which spiders deposit their eggs
59. Gulf port
61. A conflict of people's opinions
64. "Your majesty"
65. Windows with sashes
66. Send to the canvas
67. Four's inferior
68. ___ bag

Down

1. "20,000 Leagues" harpooner ___ Land
2. Again
3. #1 spot
4. The middle of the day
5. Became an issue
6. Capacity equal to 10 litres
7. All excited
8. A unit of resistance equal to one million ohms
9. Last word of "America, the Beautiful"
10. Relish
11. Cupid's projectile
12. Freshman, probably
14. Disconnected
15. Fraction of a newton
21. Said to make a horse go faster
24. Asian tongue
26. "___ Town Too" (1981 hit)
27. ___ souci
28. Beethoven's "Archduke ___"
29. Decorative needlework
31. Block house?
34. Cashew, e.g.
35. Diving bird
36. Greek earth goddess: Var.
37. Missing from the Marines, say
39. Confuse
40. Spanish appetizer
43. "Kapow!"
45. A substance that oxidizes another substance
47. Rodeo ring?
48. Saclike dilations in a compound gland
49. TV, radio, etc.
50. Brewski
52. Marked by the presence of snow
53. Take pleasure in
55. "Back in the ___"
57. Bring to ruin
58. Sean Connery, for one
60. "The Matrix" role
62. "___ Cried" (1962 hit)
63. "Concentration" pronoun

PUZZLE 15

1	2	3	4		5	6	7	8			9	10	11	12
13				14				15		16			
17										18			
	19						20			21			22		
			23			24		25			26			
27	28	29				30	31			32			
33					34				35				36	37
38				39				40				41		
42			43				44				45		
		46				47				48			
	49				50			51	52				
53				54			55		56			57	58	
59			60		61			62					63
64					65								
66						67					68		

Across

1. Little, e.g.
5. "___ who?"
9. "Enigma Variations" composer
14. Checker, perhaps
15. 1952 Olympics host
16. Left-hand page
17. Banquets
18. Clinched
19. Boot
20. Exhibiting magnetism
23. Afflict
24. Abbr. after a name
25. "What's the ___?"
26. Athletic supporter?
27. Tissue thin sheets of pastry
29. Pickpocket, in slang
32. Ancient assembly area
35. Greek letter
36. ___ list
37. A small garden where vegetables are grown
40. The "O" in S.R.O.
41. Bridge site
42. Baggy
43. ___ bit
44. Cunning
45. Boozehound
46. Black gold
47. "Walking on Thin Ice" singer
48. ___ de deux
51. Without delay
57. A rich soil
58. Banned apple spray
59. An initiation ceremony for males
60. Dark
61. Beget
62. Carbon compound
63. Big drawer?
64. Cookers
65. Newton fraction

Down

1. Bamboozled
2. Physicist who proposed the exclusion principle
3. Cough up
4. A kind of computer architecture
5. Evening do
6. English race place
7. (cosmology) the original matter
8. Fizzy drink
9. Be that as it may
10. Bank
11. Pluck
12. Fungal spore sacs
13. Campus military org.
21. Milk-Bone biscuit, e.g.
22. A Russian prison camp for political prisoners
26. It doesn't take much
27. Bad move
28. Any thing
29. Birdbrain
30. Dangerous time
31. Corn ___
32. Affirm
33. Characteristic carrier
34. Eye
35. Surefooted goat
36. Bring (out)
38. "Get ___ of yourself!"
39. Cool
44. Party
45. They're boring
46. Of or relating to or measured in ohms
47. Eyeball benders
48. Fake
49. Composer Copland
50. Flat
51. Astringent
52. Color quality
53. It's softer than gypsum
54. Coarse file
55. Medley
56. Lying, maybe

PUZZLE 16

Across

1. Announce
7. Pick, with "for"
10. Ponzi scheme, e.g.
14. Leave or strike out
15. Handle clumsily
16. About
17. Actually
20. Kosher ___
21. Appear
22. Tall perennial herb of tropical Asia
23. Old Chinese money
26. Debtor's note
28. Drivel
31. The first tier of seats above the orchestra
37. Henry Clay, for one
39. Worn to shreds
40. Word repeated after "Que"
41. Elephant's weight, maybe
42. Balcony section
43. Cineplex feature
46. A person who is not a Christian
48. Farthest to the east
50. In-flight info, for short
51. Good, in the 'hood
52. ___ Piper
54. Befuddled
58. Bauxite, e.g.
60. Penny, perhaps
64. Devoid of passion or feeling
68. Needle case
69. Chapter in history
70. Small-time dictator
71. Balance sheet item
72. Conclusion of some games
73. A belief that can guide behaviour

Down

1. Principal
2. "Anything ___?"
3. 100 dinars
4. ___ one
5. Grazing area
6. Banned insecticide
7. Crude group?
8. Devoted to a cause or party
9. Quip, part 3
10. Comfy spot
11. Jam
12. Fungal spore sacs
13. Bit of dust
18. A fisherman may spin one
19. Theme of this puzzle
24. "Much ___ About Nothing"
25. Be mistaken
27. Columbus Day mo.
28. Chasers
29. Madison Square Garden, e.g.
30. A soldier in the paratroops
32. Attack
33. Bank
34. Grimalkin
35. Kosher
36. Swelling
38. Boor's lack
41. Based on cooking in a tandoor
44. Meat cooked on a skewer
45. Car accessory
46. Telepathy, e.g.
47. Downed a sub, say
49. Kind of column
53. "La vita nuova" poet
54. Breezed through
55. Bag
56. Soft lump or unevenness in a yarn
57. Tinker with, in a way
59. Bookbinding leather
61. "I, Claudius" role
62. Boris Godunov, for one
63. Catch sight of
65. Chair part
66. "Humanum ___ errare"
67. Code word

PUZZLE 17

1	2	3	4	5	6		7	8	9		10	11	12	13
14							15				16			
17					18				19					
20						21				22				
		23	24	25			26	27						
28	29	30		31			32				33	34	35	36
37			38				39							
40					41					42				
43			44	45				46	47					
48							49				50			
			51				52		53					
54	55	56	57			58	59				60	61	62	63
64				65			66	67						
68				69			70							
71				72			73							

Across

1. Halo, e.g.
5. Prepare, as tea
10. Distress signal
14. Figurehead's place
15. Conscious
16. Fall follower
17. Russian Saint
20. Addition
21. "Planet of the ___"
22. American symbol
23. Not fake or counterfeit
24. Resembling a box in rectangularity
26. Bombed
29. Fellow
30. Harvest goddess
33. Duck's home
34. Boiled or baked buckwheat
35. ___ Dee River
36. Stunt with a revolver
40. "___ Time transfigured me": Yeats
41. Condescending one
42. "Beowulf" beverage
43. Approx.
44. Scattered
45. In an avid manner
47. 10 jiao
48. Came down
49. Bristles
52. Western blue flag, e.g.
53. Money in Moldova
56. Postpone or delay needlessly
60. Egyptian cross
61. "Silly" birds
62. "... there is no ___ angel but Love": Shakespeare
63. Convene
64. High points
65. The basic unit of money in Ghana

Down

1. ___ line (major axis of an elliptical orbit)
2. ___-Altaic languages
3. Aggravate
4. Barley bristle
5. The Greek lyric poet of Lesbos
6. Canary's call
7. Beanery sign
8. Barely get, with "out"
9. The "p" in r.p.m.
10. Cornered
11. Noise made by an engine
12. Blow chunks
13. Advantage
18. Approach
19. Characterized by sexuality
23. Aims
24. Inebriate
25. Diamond Head locale
26. Bender
27. A time period for working
28. Atlas feature
29. Nobleman
30. ___ out (declined)
31. Corolla part
32. Down at the heels
34. Famous
37. Mint, e.g.
38. Small buffalo of the Celebes
39. Give off, as light
45. Dress styles
46. MasterCard alternative
47. Marina sight
48. Come to mind
49. Junk E-mail
50. Coastal raptor
51. Drag
52. Big-ticket ___
53. In person
54. "Idylls of the King" character
55. ___ fruit
57. ___ Khan
58. "Hold on a ___!"
59. P.I., e.g.

PUZZLE 18

Across

1. Acclaim
6. Kind of account
10. "Mi chiamano Mimi," e.g.
14. Plural of "this"
15. A supernatural life force
16. Bust maker
17. College
20. Bacchanal
21. Auspices
22. Source of sesame seed and sesame oil
23. 007, for one
24. "Bye!"
25. A kind of computer architecture
26. Bamboozle
27. "___ does it!"
29. "And I Love ___"
32. Convex molding
35. Ages
36. Dolly of "Hello, Dolly!"
37. RNA
40. Duke
41. The Beatles' "___ Leaving Home"
42. Bracelet site
43. Hale
44. Grass uitable for grazing by livestock
45. Hallucinogen
46. Bust, so to speak
48. Algonquian Indian
50. Bug
53. Fertilization site
55. Benefit
56. Distinctive flair
57. A postcard with a picture on one side
60. Choir member
61. "The ___ have it"
62. A slice
63. Amount to make do with
64. "Hey ... over here!"
65. Frigid

Down

1. Character
2. Wake-up call?
3. Having long legs
4. Gray
5. Casual attire
6. Finale
7. Astronomical telescope
8. End of the alimentary canal
9. Anita Brookner's "Hotel du ___"
10. Chips in
11. Deferral
12. "Pumping ___"
13. Bad marks
18. Curb, with "in"
19. Not much
24. Masked critter
25. Doctor Who villainess, with "the"
26. Coagulate
28. Works in the garden
30. Axis of ___
31. Carnival attraction
32. "Carmina Burana" composer
33. Henry ___
34. Blocks
35. In need of a massage
36. Capture
38. Brought into play
39. Beer buy
44. In ___ of
45. Contact, e.g.
47. Choir voices
49. Fowl place
50. Swing wildly
51. Caterpillar, for one
52. Anesthetized
53. Girasol, e.g.
54. Foul
55. A title of respect for a man in Turkey
56. Audio effect
58. 50 Cent piece
59. Kitchen meas.

PUZZLE 19

Across

1. Ancient greetings
5. Shorten, in a way
8. Get-out-of-jail money
12. 100 kurus
13. In need of resupply, maybe
14. About
15. Came down to earth
16. Condo, e.g.
17. Uncertain
18. The act of entering again
20. Grayish
21. "He's ___ nowhere man" (Beatles lyric)
22. And more
23. Something of small importance
26. Divided into areolae
30. Aquarium denizen
31. Speak softly or indistinctly
34. Clip
35. A long narrow opening
37. Contents of some barrels
38. Romance, e.g.
39. Cry in a mudslinging contest
40. Enigma
42. Abet
43. The act of imputing blame or guilt
45. Not picked up
47. "The Lord of the Rings" figure
48. Object
50. Astronomical effect
52. A sighting device in an aircraft
56. "Belling the Cat" author
57. Garage job
58. Used as fertilizer
59. Desire
60. ___-friendly
61. Buster
62. Hit the bottle
63. Cabernet, e.g.
64. Edible starchy tuberous root of taro plants

Down

1. Banned orchard spray
2. Loathsome
3. Buffalo's county
4. A navigation system using orbiting satellites
5. Craze
6. Bay window
7. Dampens
8. A kind of early movie projector
9. Bow
10. Gross
11. Nonclerical
13. News office
14. Box
19. Cuts back
22. Be off
23. 10 kilogauss
24. Archaeological find
25. ___ artery
26. "___ Lang Syne"
27. Hawaiian island
28. Bitter
29. High-pitched
32. Agitate
33. ___-Atlantic
36. A person loved by another person
38. Trivial Pursuit edition
40. Churchill's "so few": Abbr.
41. Move heavily or clumsily
44. Inclination
46. Like the Godhead
48. Drench
49. Put in
50. "My ___!"
51. "Hurry!"
52. Cloud
53. Alum
54. Drove
55. ___ Bell
56. Be in a cast

PUZZLE 20

43

Across

1. Dead center?
5. Pelvic bones
10. Torn cloth
14. "Tosca" tune
15. Lace tip
16. Knowing, as a secret
17. A timid man
19. Ancient colonnade
20. A-list
21. Stunning
23. ___ chi
26. African grazer
27. A series of small amounts
34. "Frasier" actress Gilpin
36. Antiquity, in antiquity
37. Stick-on
38. Bone-dry
39. Pan, e.g.
42. Corker
43. American worker
45. Ball in a socket
46. Bit of gossip
47. Freedom from doubt
51. PC "brain"
52. Bonanza find
53. North America South America
58. Apportion
63. A lot of lot
64. Uncontrollably noisy
67. Climb
68. Aviary sound
69. Santa ___, California
70. Have the ___ for
71. A high wave caused by tidal flow
72. Rich Little, e.g.

Down

1. Bind
2. Kind of agreement
3. Peewee
4. Pieces of fabric used for stuffing or insulation
5. Adage
6. Eastern title
7. Cut short
8. Quit
9. Be there
10. A kind of computer architecture
11. The "A" of ABM
12. Continue
13. Catch
18. Abominable Snowman
22. European freshwater fish resembling the roach
24. Out, in a way
25. "Cast Away" setting
27. Practice
28. Free from
29. "Farewell, mon ami"
30. Archaeologist's find
31. Grave
32. Bundle
33. Urban blight
34. Worthless or oversimplified ideas
35. Buffalo's lake
40. Apprentice
41. Calendar span
44. Chalupa alternative
48. Make neat, smart, or trim
49. Antibacterial
50. Warm, so to speak
53. "The Turtle" poet
54. Bounce back
55. Court instrument
56. A common cyst of the skin
57. Remnant
59. Foreign currency
60. Aerial maneuver
61. Yorkshire river
62. Ivan the Terrible, e.g.
65. "___ the glad waters of the dark blue sea": Byron
66. Flatter, in a way

PUZZLE 21

Across

1. Attention ___
5. Messy dresser
9. Eye amorously
13. Garden bulb
15. Word before and after "against"
16. "Guilty," e.g.
17. Amphitheater
18. Crowd sound
19. A little night music
20. A son of your niece or nephew
23. Chester White's home
24. Ground cover
25. A ruling on a point of Islamic law
27. Debaucher
30. Stop working
32. Fast feline
33. Captured
35. British - A bundle of sticks and branches
38. Heavy, durable furniture wood
39. Hang
41. Approaching
42. Go off script
44. 100 centavos
45. Quip, part 3
46. A laminated metamorphic rock
48. Brouhaha
50. Indian melodies
51. Get a move on
52. Cheesecake ingredient?
53. People who constitute the main body of any group
60. Food thickener
62. Charged particles
63. Birch relative
64. Actress Catherine ___-Jones
65. Above
66. Angers
67. "Our Time in ___" (10,000 Maniacs album)
68. Chops
69. Kid

Down

1. Alone
2. Engine sound
3. Sheltered, at sea
4. The Babylonian goddess of the watery deep
5. Bit
6. Ankh feature
7. Brightly colored fish
8. Forlorn
9. Select, with "for"
10. An inhabitant of Glasgow
11. Has a baryon number of 0
12. "No problem"
14. Easy mark
21. Civil War side
22. Homeless child
26. Hypnotic state
27. Sought damages
28. Blend
29. Very attractive; capturing interest
30. Gads about
31. Barely gets, with "out"
32. "Harper Valley ___"
34. "My bad!"
36. Shrek, e.g.
37. Not just "a"
40. Rub onto
43. Den denizen
47. "Four Essays on Liberty" author Berlin
49. Chest material
50. Carried on
51. Secure or lock with a...
52. See stars, maybe
54. Do, for example
55. Comprehend
56. Dart
57. One way to stand by
58. Onion relative
59. European language
61. Bled

PUZZLE 22

Across

1. Sonata, e.g.
5. 1973 Supreme Court decision name
9. Big deal
12. Olympic sled
13. Beautiful people
15. All fired up
16. Bermuda, e.g.
17. For all to hear
18. Lentil, e.g.
19. Feeling self-importance
22. Lt.'s inferior, in the Navy
23. And so forth
24. Top competitors, often
28. Doctor's order
30. Eat at a restaurant
31. Assumed name
34. Binge
36. Vacation locale, with "the"
37. It is equal to the center of mass
41. International Fund
42. Bluenose
43. A floor covering
44. The back of the body of a vertebrate
47. Start of a refrain
49. Comes (to)
50. Gibbon, for one
51. Engine need
54. The conveyance of a property back to a former owner
59. "The Open Window" writer
62. Construction piece
63. Brother of Abel
64. Bit of kindling
65. Blood carrier
66. Help for the stumped
67. Appetite
68. Barbara of "I Dream of Jeannie"
69. "Cogito ___ sum"

Down

1. Antipasto morsel
2. A city in southeastern South Korea
3. Juicy hybrid between tangerine and grapefruit
4. Caught in the act
5. Fortune
6. A person with authority to deal out
7. Christian name
8. Needle holder
9. "___ Maria"
10. Expire
11. Anomalous
14. Tokyo, formerly
15. Money in the bank, say
20. Fliers in V's
21. ___ Today
25. A red fluorescent dye (Cosmetics)
26. Because of
27. Collar inserts
28. Backstabber
29. Suit
30. Be off base
31. Litmus reddeners
32. Sprite flavor
33. Prefix with red
35. Make worse
38. Engine speed, for short
39. Back street
40. ___ Appia
45. Bit of parsley
46. Finish, with "up"
48. Missing Link
51. Kind of personality
52. Cake topper
53. Slow, musically
55. It has moles: Abbr.
56. "O" in old radio lingo
57. Doofus
58. Flu symptom
59. Dump
60. Cow, maybe
61. Connections

PUZZLE 23

Across

1. Abbey area
5. Break off
10. Book after Joel
14. Actor Pitt
15. Bind
16. Back of the neck
17. Furnace fuel
18. Acadia National Park locale
19. Computer picture
20. Any accounting periods of 12 months
23. All ___
24. Rinse, as with a solvent
25. An instrument used to make tracings
29. ___ President
32. ___ carotene
33. Office papers
34. Ballpark fig.
37. A private detective employed by a merchant
41. Dash
42. Aired again
43. Italian bread
44. Categorize
45. A social or business visitor
47. Black ink item
50. Coal carrier
51. The 60th wedding anniversary
58. "I'm ___ you!"
59. Gasket
60. Advertising sign
62. Annoyance
63. Social
64. Algonquian language
65. Baby
66. Animal in a roundup
67. Emcee

Down

1. "20/20" network
2. University highest ranking faculty
3. "Tobermory" writer
4. Costar of TV's "How to Marry a Millionaire"
5. United States sociologist (1840-1910)
6. Legislate
7. Henry ___
8. "Empedocles on ___" (Matthew Arnold poem)
9. Country dance
10. Founder of Scholasticism
11. A former Portuguese province on the south coast of China
12. Eyeball benders
13. Taste, e.g.
21. Amaze
22. Bakery supply
25. Cookbook abbr.
26. A network of intersecting blood vessels
27. At the peak of
28. "Wheels"
29. Nickel, e.g.
30. "Absolutely!"
31. Elmer, to Bugs
33. ___ mortals
34. Bad to the bone
35. Arid
36. Nicholas II, for one
38. Daughter of Mnemosyne
39. Center of a ball?
40. Calamity
44. Tart
45. An amusingly eccentric old man
46. Annex
47. Assume
48. 1967 war locale
49. Audited, with "on"
50. Beginning of a conclusion
52. Acceptances
53. "Dang!"
54. Soave, e.g.
55. Mark of a ruler
56. Adopted son of Claudius
57. Functions
61. After-tax amount

PUZZLE 24

Across

1. Jam-pack
5. "Odyssey" enchantress
10. Cram, with "up"
14. French novelist Pierre
15. Arctic ___
16. Comply with
17. Bothers
18. Relating to or resembling a cone
19. Old stories
20. Used of nonindulgent persons
23. Salk's conquest
24. Can you dig it?
25. Courtroom event
29. Barely make
34. "___ to Joy"
37. Courtyards
39. "Green Gables" girl
40. Data - Births, Deaths, Medical, Marriages
44. "-zoic" things
45. Dorm annoyance
46. "Sesame Street" watcher
47. Wrestling hold
50. Amorphous creature
52. Ballpoint, e.g.
54. Dark area
58. Accomplished Fact
64. Clash of clans
65. Band
66. Congers
67. Benjamin Disraeli, e.g.
68. Sierra ___
69. A rapid series of short loud sounds
70. Highlands hillside
71. Big Bertha's birthplace
72. At one time, at one time

Down

1. Catch
2. Isuzu model
3. Bikini, for one
4. Someone unable to adapt to their circumstances
5. Chanel of fashion
6. Computer image
7. Cost of living?
8. Where "Aida" premiered
9. "More!"
10. The rounded seed-bearing capsule of a cotton
11. ___ d'amore
12. Dork
13. Cataract site
21. Reef material
22. 100 qintars
26. "___ De-Lovely"
27. Song and dance, e.g.
28. Jungle climber
30. "Have some"
31. "Don't bet ___!"
32. To a remarkable degree or extent
33. Midterm, e.g.
34. Baker's need
35. Acute
36. Abbr. at the end of a list
38. Bit
41. Biblical beast
42. Anger
43. Moistens and protects the skin
48. Be decisive
49. Get cozy
51. Current amount
53. Holes in the head
55. Bedim
56. A small stream
57. Good point
58. Alarm
59. A celebrity may have one
60. Empty
61. Whispers sweet nothings
62. Christmas decoration
63. Airy
64. Presidents' Day mo.

PUZZLE 25

1	2	3	4		5	6	7	8	9		10	11	12	13
14					15						16			
17					18						19			
20				21						22				
23							24							
			25		26	27	28		29		30	31	32	33
34	35	36		37				38			39			
40			41						42	43				
44					45							46		
47				48	49		50				51			
			52		53				54			55	56	57
	58	59	60			61	62	63						
64					65						66			
67					68						69			
70					71						72			

Across

1. End
4. "M*A*S*H" role
9. ___ President
14. Biochemistry abbr.
15. Philippine banana tree
16. Accused's need
17. "Rocks"
18. Marina sight
19. Bedouin
20. A certificate saying that a departing ship's company is healthy
23. State capital and largest city of Georgia
24. A camp defended by a circular formation of wagons
28. "Laughable Lyrics" writer
29. Couch
32. "___ here"
33. Engage in passive relaxation
36. Attention
38. Blazer, e.g.
39. One of the four pointed conical teeth
42. I, to Claudius
44. Downer
45. Clinch, with "up"
46. Disease cause
48. Pair
50. Frosts, as a cake
54. Agreeable
56. Come (from)
59. Reasonable care taken by a person to avoid harm
62. Hinder
65. Tomato blight
66. Electrical unit
67. Newswoman Shriver
68. Adjust
69. Aquatic shocker
70. Tangle
71. Demands
72. Arid

Down

1. Relating to or characteristic of a tribe
2. Egg on
3. Spanish dish
4. A synthetic silklike fabric
5. To the rear
6. Russian country house
7. Have a hankering
8. Pro ___
9. Kind of ray
10. Warm welcomes
11. Faint
12. "The ___ Daba Honeymoon"
13. Central
21. Cocoon contents
22. South American plains
25. Cut
26. Big bird
27. Gun, as an engine
30. Last letter
31. In shape
34. Armageddon
35. An encircling or ringlike structure
37. ___-eyed
39. Oil source
40. "Uh-uh"
41. Bale binder
42. Bird-to-be
43. "Fancy that!"
47. Some point in the air; above ground level
49. Computer key
51. Small and light boat
52. Goya, for one
53. Suitable
55. Acoustic
57. Played charades
58. A colloidal extract of algae
60. Campus bigwig
61. Groundless
62. Dash lengths
63. "Holy smokes!"
64. Car protector

PUZZLE 26

Across

1. Grinding powder to dust
5. Particular, for short
9. Cram
14. Small buffalo of the Celebes
15. A head
16. Rage
17. Catch with a net
18. Turkish honorific
19. Take up space
20. An unshakable belief
23. Court figure
24. Attention
25. Eagerness
29. Not alert
34. Check
37. Wound by piercing
39. Blows it
40. Natives of USA
44. Persian spirit
45. Hawaiian veranda
46. Arrange
47. Sweater material
50. OK, in a way
52. "___ magic!"
54. A stack of hay
58. Independent contractor
64. Cactus having yellow flowers
65. Mozart's "Il mio tesoro," e.g.
66. "Not guilty," e.g.
67. Best of the best
68. Sonatas, e.g.
69. Misfortunes
70. Kitchen gadget
71. The basic unit of money in Myanmar
72. Does

Down

1. Power, authority; a supernatural life force
2. Dead to the world
3. Singer Lenya
4. A female Latin American
5. Close, as an envelope
6. Leaf unit
7. Canyon effect
8. Irritate
9. Maybelline mishaps
10. 2004 Queen Latifah movie
11. Newton, e.g.
12. Drop a line?
13. ___ Tuesday (Mardi Gras)
21. Literally, "dwarf dog"
22. J.F.K. overseer
26. A dwarf
27. Kind of exam
28. Kidney-related
30. Floral ring
31. Ages
32. Marine eagle
33. "Hey there!"
34. Spanish snack
35. "I'll second that"
36. "Lulu" composer
38. Banquet
41. "Flying Down to ___"
42. Henpeck
43. A personal journal
48. One who rifles; a robber
49. Took the cake, say
51. Clear
53. Buss
55. Quartet member
56. Genuflected
57. Hiding place
58. Arias, usually
59. "Beowulf," for one
60. When repeated, like some shows
61. Beseech
62. Italian money
63. Brewer's equipment
64. "Waking ___ Devine" (1998 film)

PUZZLE 27

Across

1. House
5. Style of rock music with gloomy lyrics
9. Bound
13. Cornstarch brand
14. Yorkshire river
15. Secretary, at times
16. The growing of vegetables or flowers for market
19. CBS logo
20. 1922 Physics Nobelist
21. ___ a high note
22. Except
23. Walk in water
24. English poet who introduced the sonnet (1503-1542)
27. Cause of inflation?
28. The Babylonian goddess of the watery deep
32. A voluptuously beautiful young woman
33. An unusually small individual
35. Disney dwarf
36. Ready for battle
39. An end to sex?
40. At attention
41. Hint
42. Grass uitable for grazing by livestock
44. Baseball bat wood
45. Mouthing off
46. Address, esp. an email address
48. Hawaiian garland
49. Magical wish granter
51. In ___ of (replacing)
52. Cable network
55. Create atmosphere
58. Carnivorous larva of lacewing flies
59. Arch type
60. Experienced
61. Brightly colored
62. Frau's partner
63. "What are the ___?"

Down

1. Bar order, with "the"
2. Cafeteria carrier
3. Shrek, for one
4. Stir-fry pan
5. Move out of or depart from
6. Should, with "to"
7. Peter the Great, e.g.
8. ___ Royal Highness
9. Deciduous trees of the genus Tilia
10. Mélange
11. ___ Station
12. .0000001 joule
15. Manage
17. State of decline
18. "Goodness!"
23. An isle and county of southern England
24. Egg: Prefix
25. Scrumptious
26. "___ we having fun yet?"
27. Common aspiration
29. "Don't get any funny ___!"
30. Score
31. Hurt
32. Acclaim
33. Literature in metrical form
34. A silvery metallic element
37. Business person
38. "Able was I ___ ..."
43. Penetrated
45. Tributary
47. Pad
48. Lid or lip application
49. Be slack-jawed
50. Canyon sound
51. Olympic sled
52. Drew on
53. Canned as sardines in Norway
54. "Hamlet" has five
55. Blackout
56. "___ la la!"
57. Amateur video subject, maybe

PUZZLE 28

1	2	3	4		5	6	7	8		9	10	11	12
13					14				15				
16				17				18					
19				20				21					
			22				23						
	24	25	26			27			28	29	30	31	
32					33			34		35			
36				37				38					
39				40				41					
42			43		44			45					
		46	47			48							
	49	50			51				52	53	54		
55				56				57					
58				59				60					
61				62				63					

59

Across

1. Deep-six
6. "___ the night before ..."
10. Lions' prey
14. Certain Arab
15. Door fastener
16. Milieu for Lemieux
17. ___ Carlo
18. Houston university
19. ___ Minor
20. Bacterial infection drugs
22. "Cool!"
23. Fifth, e.g.: Abbr.
24. Set aflame
26. (music) play at low speed
30. Literature in metrical form
32. Enraged
33. Fraternity letter
34. Canton neighbor
38. Arabian Peninsula country
39. "How exciting!"
40. Finger, in a way
41. A soft oily clay used as a pigment
43. "___ show time!"
44. Place
45. Yo-Yo Ma's instrument
47. Sacred songs
48. Unwind from or as if from a reel
51. Campaigner, for short
52. Cart
53. The 3rd syllable of a word counting back from the end
60. Challenge, metaphorically
61. Phobos, to Mars
62. Craze
63. Eye layer
64. Indian tourist city
65. Like some walls
66. German mister
67. Dirty
68. Large constellation on the equator near Pisces and Aquarius

Down

1. "Brave New World" drug
2. "Follow me!"
3. Bluster
4. Voting "no"
5. A spotted or calico horse or pony
6. Pang
7. "Hold it!"
8. Fungal spore sacs
9. Coin
10. A reef knot crossed the wrong way
11. Japanese-American
12. A member of the Uniat Church
13. Fish that lays an egg case called a mermaid's purse
21. Brown, e.g.
25. Fed. property manager
26. Neatnik's opposite
27. Airport pickup
28. Elliptical
29. Storage space
30. It's a snap
31. ___ and aahs
33. Disturb
35. Level, in London
36. Bypass
37. Brings home
42. "Didn't I tell you?"
44. Dispute or controversy
46. Andean animals
47. Finish, with "up"
48. "Yeah"
49. Green
50. King or queen
51. Kind of code
54. Canceled
55. Spelling of "Beverly Hills 90210"
56. Church part
57. Newton, for one
58. Place
59. Boys

PUZZLE 29

Across

1. 1990 World Series champs
5. Symbol of authority
10. Alpine transport
14. Brilliantly colored fish
15. Archaeological site
16. Bill Clinton's birthplace
17. Calf-length skirt
18. Bailiwicks
19. Some deer
20. Spanish adventurer
23. Air bag?
24. "Silent Night" adjective
25. Euripides drama
28. Attorneys' org.
31. Choppers, so to speak
35. Anxiety
37. "To Autumn," e.g.
39. By means of
40. Improving yourself
44. International Fund
45. Big coffee holder
46. Display
47. "Here!"
50. "Are we there ___?"
52. Bridge positions
53. "For ___ a jolly ..."
55. Achilles, e.g.
57. Same genetics
63. Long
64. Lacquer ingredient
65. "I had no ___!"
67. Big pig
68. Broadcast
69. "Cheers" regular
70. As recently as
71. Parsonage
72. Hardly haute cuisine

Down

1. CD follower
2. "Paradise Lost," e.g.
3. Pedestal part
4. Used formerly for shinplasters
5. Von of the space race
6. Constellation between Great Bear and Orion
7. Fizzles out
8. Buzzing pest
9. English exam finale, often
10. Seat of power
11. Philistine
12. Big galoots
13. ___ gestae
21. Seeming
22. "i" lid
25. Singers and instruments
26. Injection to stimulate evacuation
27. Dutch pottery city
29. Carried
30. Big fuss
32. Balances
33. Add color to
34. Abominates
36. Cousin of an ostrich
38. Role in Haydn's "The Creation"
41. Be nosy
42. Flip
43. Cat-like sound
48. Chipper
49. Egg maker
51. London river
54. Cook, as clams
56. Say "Li'l Abner," say
57. Computer symbol
58. Indian dish made with stewed legumes
59. Hip bones
60. Nuclear research
61. TV's "American ___"
62. Agrippina's slayer
63. Blood-typing letters
66. Band aid

PUZZLE 30

63

Across

1. Locker room supply
5. Big story
9. 100 lbs.
12. Side squared, for a square
13. Burgundy grape
15. Be different
16. Wrong direction
18. Arabic for "commander"
19. "Mangia!"
20. Deep
21. Regarding this point
23. Coal site
24. Breezy
25. Can't stand
28. Bubbling sound
32. Black cat, to some
33. Abrupt
34. "The very ___!"
35. "Schindler's ___"
36. Met expectations?
37. Demoiselle
38. Earthen pot
39. Nasty
40. Loiter
41. Same time
43. Make stout
45. ___ tide
46. Poor Hygiene
47. Above the collarbone
50. Chamber group, maybe
51. Ed.'s request
54. Beat badly
55. Used on the high seas
58. Capri, e.g.
59. Change, chemically
60. Against
61. "Gosh!"
62. Some Olympians, nowadays
63. Charges

Down

1. Break
2. Mozart's "Madamina," e.g.
3. "___ we forget"
4. Bounder
5. Electronic publication
6. Allotment
7. Move slowly
8. Bunk
9. Amounted (to)
10. Court order
11. Beginner
14. Vacation souvenirs
15. A coloured flare fired from a Very pistol
17. Camera diaphragm
22. A little bit of work
23. Intent to remember
24. Surrounding glows
25. Grief
26. "South Pacific" hero
27. Edison contemporary
28. Cunning
29. Dostoyevsky novel, with "The"
30. Audacity
31. Greek anatomist (medicine)
33. Hamper
36. Ace
42. 1773 jetsam
43. Lacking clarity or distinctness
44. Awestruck
46. Harsh Athenian lawgiver
47. H.S. class
48. Cheat, slangily
49. Be a monarch
50. Drop from Niobe
51. ___ function
52. Some chips, maybe
53. Auspices: Var.
56. A large edible mushroom with a brown cap
57. Bonehead

PUZZLE 31

1	2	3	4		5	6	7	8				9	10	11
12					13				14		15			
16				17							18			
19					20					21	22			
			23						24					
25	26	27					28					29	30	31
32						33					34			
35					36						37			
38					39						40			
41				42					43	44				
			45					46						
47	48	49					50					51	52	53
54					55	56					57			
58					59						60			
61					62						63			

Across

1. Aircraft compartment
4. Certain herring
8. Brown ermine
13. Charlotte-to-Raleigh dir.
14. Star
16. Kind of dog
17. Newcomer, briefly
18. Bowl
19. Archeologist's find
20. System response
23. Colossal
24. Morgue, for one
25. "The Sweetheart of Sigma ___"
28. Your grandmother
29. Very, in music
32. Fall sound
33. Religious law
35. Conservative
37. Rivalry
40. Accord or comport with
41. Laugh-a-minute folks
42. All over
43. "Come here ___?"
45. Formerly, formerly
49. Chain letters?
50. Boiling blood
51. Intense
52. Artificial digestion
56. Press
59. ___ manual
60. Affirmative action
61. Heretofore
62. Feather, zoologically
63. Bigheadedness
64. About 1.3 cubic yards
65. Check
66. Animal house

Down

1. Harmless
2. Lack of vigor
3. Cultivated his own land
4. Barely enough
5. "Catch!"
6. Brews
7. Contradict
8. Sloping mass of loose rocks
9. Not us
10. Flattery
11. "Aladdin" prince
12. ___-tac-toe
15. Iraqi port
21. Turn
22. A price to pay
25. À la mode
26. Colors
27. Driver's lic. and others
29. From now on
30. Bribe
31. Belt
32. 3
34. Bolted down
36. His "4" was retired
37. Brown alternative
38. Fishing, perhaps
39. Fabrication
40. Defective
44. Disgusted
46. Devastated
47. Butt of jokes
48. Sinew
50. About to explode
51. Indian state
52. Dock
53. Egyptian fertility goddess
54. Chap
55. Marine flier
56. Bell and Barker
57. Best guess: Abbr.
58. Blonde's secret, maybe

PUZZLE 32

Across
1. Fluorocarbon with chlorine
4. "When it's ___" (old riddle answer)
8. Jersey, e.g.
12. Narc's find, perhaps
13. Ancient alphabetic character
14. Edmonton hockey player
16. Camera part
17. Broadcast
18. Safari sight
19. "Able was I ___."
20. Blueprint
21. Fall flat
23. Broke bread
24. Artistic quality
26. Cold and wet
28. Conceit
30. Drone, e.g.
32. Mythology anthology
36. Sacred Hindu writings
39. Country ID
41. Informal, BBC
42. Christian ___
43. Island nation east of Fiji
45. Bass, e.g.
46. Cabal
48. Have a sudden inspiration?
49. Trim to fit, maybe
50. Squire
51. Fa follower
52. ___ Grove Village, Ill.
54. "___ rang?"
56. Eagle's home
60. "My man!"
63. Hawaiian wreath
65. Cut
67. Down Under bird
68. Drunk, in slang
70. Become unhinged
72. Asterisk
73. Cover story?
74. Ancestry
75. "Cogito, ___ sum"
76. Brain area
77. Enthusiasm
78. Court

Down
1. Sky sight
2. Ace
3. Comedian Bill, informally
4. Acreage
5. Enter eagerly
6. "Wheel of Fortune" buy
7. Abbr. after many a general's name
8. 1988 Olympics locale
9. Health Authority
10. Hipbones
11. Camping gear
12. Capital on the Dnieper
15. 1973 Supreme Court decision name
20. Kind of shot
22. Burn up
25. Caffeine source
27. Fly catcher
29. "How ___ Has the Banshee Cried" (Thomas Moore poem)
30. Far from fresh
31. Baker's dozen?
33. Gone
34. New York's Carnegie ___
35. "Not on ___!" ("No way!")
36. Hop, skip or jump
37. Canal of song
38. "Two Years Before the Mast" writer
40. Apple's apple, e.g.
44. King Kong, e.g.
47. Chap
49. Barely make, with "out"
51. "So ___ me!"
53. Bar topic
55. Blast from the past
57. Back in
58. Insect stage
59. 100 cents
60. ___ constrictor
61. Brook
62. Miscellany
64. Capri, for one
65. A supernatural life force
66. Available
69. Decline
71. Common soccer score
72. Finalize, with "up"

PUZZLE 33

Across

1. "___ Doubtfire"
4. Short order, for short
7. Colorful fish
11. "Bye"
12. Mishmash
13. Large intenstine cavity
15. Shaking
17. Start of a refrain
18. Calendar abbr.
19. Clear
21. When it's broken, that's good
22. Layer
23. Ancient greetings
24. Certain tide
27. "___ moment"
28. Young raptor
30. Gulf V.I.P.
33. Caroled
36. Arctic
38. Bee ___
39. Hilo garland
40. Nolo contendere, e.g.
41. Burning
43. Baja bread
45. Do damage to
46. Spousal connection
48. Inflammation
50. Coin featuring Leonardo da Vinci's Vitruvian Man
51. Increase, with "up"
53. Advantages
56. Fat letters
58. Dragon
60. The Smothers Brothers, e.g.
61. Twangy, as a voice
64. No influence
66. Swelling
67. Celeb
68. Infinitesimal amount
69. Glimpse
70. ___ Aviv
71. Farm area

Down

1. Any sound resembling a cat meow
2. Long-limbed
3. Groundskeeper's supply
4. Hold responsible
5. Defective speech
6. A lightweight hat worn
7. Critical campaign mo.
8. The "p" of m.p.h.
9. Without instrument
10. Kind of skirt
11. Crack, in a way
12. Black or green
14. Fold, spindle or mutilate
16. Extended family
20. Genetic stuff
25. Bloke
26. Hebrew letters
27. Brass
28. Protection
29. Bank
30. Dr. J's first pro league
31. O. Henry's "The Gift of the ___"
32. Bad feelings
34. "The Sound of Music" backdrop
35. Alumna bio word
37. Beaver's work
42. "This means ___!"
44. First act
47. Moo goo gai pan pan
49. "Once ___ a time..."
51. Walloped, old-style
52. Variations
53. Blockhead
54. Bats
55. ___ bean
56. Chemical ending
57. Fabricated
59. Acad.
62. Band aid?
63. Nonprofessional
65. "___ the season ..."

PUZZLE 34

Across

1. Catch, as flies
5. 1952 Olympics site
9. Drawn
14. Andean land
15. Coffee choice
16. ___ dark space (region in a vacuum tube)
17. Husk
18. McDonald's arches, e.g.
19. Hyperion, for one
20. Personal prize
23. Coast Guard officer: Abbr.
24. Big wine holder
25. "___ luck?"
26. Kind of mill
27. "I'm ___ your tricks!"
29. It was dropped in the 60's
32. Swiss capital
35. "Shoo!"
36. Sky box?
37. Relative clause
40. Whence the Magi, with "the"
41. Eat
42. Copper
43. Tokyo, once
44. Boosts
45. "Holy cow!"
46. All-___
47. Sticker
48. Inflammation
51. Against ideals
57. Auctioneer's word
58. Base
59. Band with the hit "Barbie Girl"
60. Ground
61. It may be due on a duplex
62. Engine sound
63. "Darn!"
64. Black
65. Enlivens, with "up"

Down

1. "The final frontier"
2. Graceful bird
3. Seed coverings
4. Deceive
5. "The Wizard of Oz" prop
6. British author of historical novels
7. Building block
8. Bouquet
9. Barrio resident
10. Accord
11. Automatic
12. ___ cheese
13. Animal shelters
21. Kick out
22. Mythical creature
26. Itsy-bitsy biter
27. Clive
28. Place to be picked up?
29. Animal with a mane
30. Bowl over
31. Controvert
32. At liberty
33. Go through
34. "Not to mention ..."
35. Ardent
36. "Trick" joint
38. Going to the dogs, e.g.
39. "La Bohème," e.g.
44. In order
45. Innocent until
46. It's spotted in westerns
47. On the
48. Nettle
49. Appropriate
50. Great balls of fire
51. A long time
52. Wyle of "ER"
53. Novice
54. Prefix with scope or meter
55. 20-20, e.g.
56. Arctic native

PUZZLE 35

1	2	3	4		5	6	7	8		9	10	11	12	13
14					15					16				
17					18					19				
20				21					22					
23					24					25				
			26				27	28				29	30	31
32	33	34				35					36			
37					38					39				
40					41					42				
43				44					45					
			46					47				48	49	50
51	52	53				54	55				56			
57						58					59			
60						61					62			
63						64					65			

Across

1. Avian chatterbox
6. Dresden's river
10. Artist Bonheur
14. Convex molding
15. Be itinerant
16. Partner of "done with"
17. Joan Rivers
20. Popular
21. Long (for)
22. Ear-related
23. Personals, e.g.
24. Breakfast staple
25. Curved molding
26. "The Joy Luck Club" author
27. Chow
29. Store convenience, for short
32. Doll
35. "Hey you!"
36. Ancient gathering place
37. Figure it out
40. "___ It Romantic?"
41. General assembly?
42. Chew (on)
43. "Awesome!"
44. Crosby, Stills and Nash, e.g.
45. Flair, e.g.
46. Wood sorrels
48. Broadway brightener
50. 30-day mo.
53. Book of maps
55. Peter, e.g.
56. Biblical birthright seller
57. Without delay
60. Used as fertilizer
61. Sundae topper, perhaps
62. "Halt!" to a salt
63. ___-American
64. Cousin of a gull
65. Force units

Down

1. Coffee shop order
2. Duck
3. Charges
4. Charity
5. Anguish
6. "All My Children" vixen
7. Nessie
8. Bottom
9. Easily tamed bird
10. Scalawag
11. Too much
12. Word repeated after "Que," in song
13. Organic radical
18. Mountain pool
19. Torn cloth
24. Dig
25. "Beetle Bailey" dog
26. Ex-lax?
28. Pale
30. Rigid necklace
31. Beat to a pulp
32. Ado
33. "Major" animal
34. Boatman
35. "Frasier" actress Gilpin
36. Flabbergast
38. 1968 Chemistry Nobelist Onsager
39. Gathering clouds, say
44. Charge
45. Go (over)
47. Chocolate source
49. Big name in stationery
50. Associated with terrorism
51. Antiquated
52. Corrodes
53. Blue hue
54. Gang land
55. Radial, e.g.
56. "Men always hate most what they ___ most": Mencken
58. Derived form of "wit"
59. "Dear old" guy

PUZZLE 36

Across

1. 1968 hit "Harper Valley ___"
4. Lift
8. Civil rights activist Parks
12. Stooge
13. Bind
14. Ally
16. Cast-of-thousands film
17. Surveyor's map
18. Newspaper department
19. Afghani money
20. Bit
21. Diminish
23. Long, long time
24. Chip dip
26. ___ grass
28. Couple
30. Kind of operation
32. Catcall
36. Open carriage
39. Peter, for one
41. A deadly sin
42. Hardly a beauty
43. Beat
45. A large edible mushroom with a brown cap
46. Guinness and others
48. Children's ___
49. Heredity carrier
50. Dumb cluck
51. "Baloney!"
52. Asian capital
54. ___ green
56. Care for
60. "Nice!"
63. "The Catcher in the ___"
65. Something to chew
67. "Hee ___"
68. Mix-up
70. Big time?
72. Information unit
73. In a lather
74. Coaster
75. Arab chieftain
76. Collapsed
77. Edible starchy tuberous root of taro plants
78. Gymnast's goal

Down

1. ___ New Guinea
2. Diagonal weave
3. Mandela's org.
4. Dittography, e.g.
5. Hightail it
6. Blotter letters
7. A network of intersecting blood vessels
8. Cuban dance
9. "A Chorus Line" number
10. Locale
11. 60's do
12. Livens (up)
15. Hither's partner
20. Moose ___, Saskatchewan
22. Constrictor
25. Farm pen
27. Café alternative
29. Baseball's Master Melvin
30. Addition symbol
31. Flatten, in a way
33. "___ bitten, twice shy"
34. Bread maker
35. Sort
36. Cousin of a herring
37. Ring
38. Ancient
40. Jerk
44. Accept
47. Drench
49. Animal with curved horns
51. 2004 nominee
53. Bankrupt
55. Blow
57. Sounds similar
58. Gown material
59. Ablutionary vessel
60. Bat wood
61. All over again
62. "Unimaginable as ___ in Heav'n": Milton
64. "___ on Down the Road"
65. Like The Citadel, now
66. Cancel
69. Good times
71. Antiquity, once
72. "Wanna ___?"

PUZZLE 37

Across
1. Amigo
4. Roll
7. Baseball stats
11. Alleviate
12. ___ lily
13. Civilian clothes
15. Duck-like features
17. Juicy hybrid between tangerine and grapefruit
18. U.N. arm
19. Turns back, perhaps
21. Branch
22. Small bird
23. Pasty-faced
24. Big East team
27. Big Apple attraction, with "the"
28. Gun cleaner
30. Barely beat
33. Floating, perhaps
36. Mischief-maker
38. Go through volumes
39. Hula hoop?
40. Coffin stand
41. 4:1, e.g.
43. Secret
45. White chip, often
46. Modify
48. Danger to divers
50. Old 45 player
51. Kind of history
53. Do-it-yourselfer's purchase
56. Buddy
58. Alcove
60. Tribute, of sorts
61. Not well throat
64. 1821 independance from Spain
66. Very, in music
67. Comrade in arms
68. Inn inventory
69. Canine cry
70. Headlight setting
71. Toni Morrison's "___ Baby"

Down
1. Physicist who proposed the exclusion principle
2. Fancy tie
3. Albanian coin
4. Wales
5. (Scottish) aside; askew
6. Biblical verb
7. It'll never fly
8. Persian, e.g.
9. Carcinogen, bioweapon
10. Arouse
11. Blue-pencil
12. Reason to close up shop
14. Any doctrine
16. Scottish hillside
20. Masseur's workplace, maybe
25. Babysitter's handful
26. Relating to or characteristic of a tribe
27. Noble Italian family name
28. Epitome of thinness
29. Losing proposition?
30. Blow it
31. "___ me!"
32. At a gateway
34. Buttonhole, e.g.
35. Bard's nightfall
37. "Maid of Athens, ___ we part": Byron
42. Buffoon
44. Frothy
47. "Dear" one
49. "If all ___ fails ..."
51. Eyes
52. Camelot, to Arthur
53. Aussie "bear"
54. Do-nothing
55. After-dinner selection
56. Hidden means of support?
57. Like Santa's cheeks
59. "Heavens to Betsy!"
62. "For Me and My ___"
63. Cool
65. "Welcome" site

PUZZLE 38

Across

1. Revenuers
5. "Hey!"
9. Sparkle
14. Gumbo ingredient
15. Moonfish
16. A Hindu sage
17. Fibber
18. Ad headline
19. (Hinduism) The soul; one's true self
20. Dramatic intervals
23. Back
24. North Sea diver
25. Evil spirit
26. Blunder
27. Hamster's home
29. Clock standard: Abbr.
32. Be bombastic
35. Chief
36. Atlas stat
37. Variety of stuff
40. Keats creations
41. Engine attachment
42. Monopoly purchase
43. Bacillus shape
44. Garment extending from the waist to the knee
45. A mother's address
46. Debate side
47. Audience
48. Blockhead
51. Shyness
57. Coronet
58. Crèche trio
59. "What've you been ___?"
60. Oust
61. Shakespeare, the Bard of ___
62. All the rage
63. Donnybrook
64. Department store department
65. Coil

Down

1. A thin layer or stratum of rock
2. Squeezing (out)
3. Harsh Athenian lawgiver
4. Indian dress
5. Charlatan
6. Hit bottom?
7. Highway department supply
8. "___-Team"
9. Metric weight
10. Very drunk
11. Doctrines
12. Bangkok native
13. Brass component
21. Risk taker
22. Theme of this puzzle
26. Greek H's
27. Salad green
28. Bad spots?
29. Small cave
30. A ___ pittance
31. Old Chinese money
32. Carbon monoxide's lack
33. Change the decor
34. Acted like
35. Crazily
36. Bit of physics
38. Acknowledge
39. Emmy-winning Lewis
44. Be generous
45. Skilled
46. "Odyssey" sorceress
47. Encourage
48. Beginning
49. Arrive, as darkness
50. Take
51. Cut off
52. Busy place
53. Racetrack fence
54. Muslim holy man
55. Church section
56. "That hurt!"

PUZZLE 39

1	2	3	4		5	6	7	8		9	10	11	12	13
14					15					16				
17					18					19				
20			21				22							
23			24				25							
		26				27	28				29	30	31	
32	33	34			35					36				
37			38					39						
40			41				42							
43			44				45							
		46			47			48	49	50				
51	52	53			54	55			56					
57				58				59						
60				61				62						
63				64				65						

81

Across

1. TV monitor?
4. 60's hairdo
8. Metric weight
12. Brand, in a way
13. Aspersion
14. Adult insect
16. Four gills
17. Campsite sight
18. Chose
19. Back then
20. Half a dozen
21. Cut
23. "If only ___ listened ..."
24. ___ preview
26. Not clerical
28. Fix, in a way
30. Lulu
32. Eye rakishly
36. Debatable
39. Ball material
41. Proper ___
42. Assist
43. Antler point
45. It would
46. Comprehend
48. Big butte
49. Aces, sometimes
50. Gumbo pod
51. Belief
52. Crash site?
54. "My dear man"
56. Aden's land
60. Software program, briefly
63. Green, in a way
65. Fanciful story
67. Alicia of "Falcon Crest"
68. People
70. Battery fluid
72. Chicken ___
73. Blender button
74. ___ of the above
75. Many elms
76. Apartment
77. Forum wear
78. Fed. property overseer

Down

1. Affect
2. Birchbark
3. Computer monitor, for short
4. ___ Spumante
5. Bend
6. Bolt
7. Crumbs
8. Plains Indian
9. Little devil
10. Homebuilder's strip
11. Double curve
12. Fitness centers
15. Eccentric
20. Go downhill fast?
22. Matterhorn, e.g.
25. "If the ___ is concealed, it succeeds": Ovid
27. Over there
29. Cheat
30. Introduction
31. Getaway spots
33. Enter
34. Vermeer's "Woman With a ___"
35. Bounds
36. Ocean menace
37. Farm call
38. Effluvium
40. Kind of dealer
44. Breach
47. Is in the past?
49. Ben Jonson wrote one to himself
51. Choler
53. Affirmative vote
55. Map feature
57. Posts
58. Injection to stimulate evacuation
59. Dark blue
60. Cleopatra biter
61. Thick cushion
62. Knit stitch
64. Covet
65. Diminutive suffix
66. Concept
69. Grazing ground
71. Bill and ___
72. Bar order

PUZZLE 40

Across
1. Holiday drink
4. Heroin, slangily
8. Blemish
12. "Where the heart is"
13. Language of Lahore
14. Well-defined
16. Cooker
17. Au ___
18. Depth charge target
19. Compensation
21. Part of BYO
23. Just
24. Grazing locale
25. War losers, usually
27. "___ the land of the free ..."
29. Archaeological site
30. ___ and cheese
31. "Seinfeld" uncle
34. German leader, Willy
37. Computer list
38. Funny
39. Itty bit
40. Many, many moons
41. Descartes's "therefore"
42. Nigerian language
43. Oil source
45. Boundary
47. "Losing My Religion" rock group
48. Aggravate
49. Bite
50. Check for accuracy
51. Wan
52. Grade A item
55. Flimsy, as an excuse
58. "Awright!"
60. Arc lamp gas
62. Offensive smell
64. Smidgen
66. Indian music
67. Calf
68. Fishing site
69. Load
70. Engine knock
71. ___ meridiem
72. Electric ___

Down
1. Star bursts
2. Last of a series
3. Heredity unit
4. Banquet
5. Color
6. "Bye"
7. Know-it-all
8. Kind of shot
9. Done for wage
10. Soon, to a bard
11. Prosperity
12. Holler
15. Farm structure
20. Fastener
22. Horse color
26. Dorothy Parker quality
28. It'll never get off the ground
29. Biology class abbr.
30. Egg protector
31. "___ of the Flies"
32. Border
33. Emanation
34. Coffin stand
35. Harassed
36. Bohr's study
37. Delivery person?
40. Antlered animal
41. A little work
43. Quiche, e.g.
44. Affectedly creative
45. "Humph!"
46. Black stone
49. Casual top
50. Within venom
51. Early priest
52. Related maternally
53. "Taras Bulba" author
54. Vex, with "at"
55. Hallucinogen
56. At the summit of
57. Epiphany figures
59. Old Icelandic literary work
61. European tongue
63. Beer barrel
65. "Ciao!"

PUZZLE 41

Across

1. Is no longer
4. C.E.O.'s degree
7. Soft mineral
11. Holdback
12. Pastrami purveyor
13. As a whole
15. Not opinionated
17. Digress
18. Bearded antelope
19. Exit
21. Bar order
22. "Casablanca" pianist
23. Crowning
24. Visored cap
27. Kind of strap
28. Dye with wax
30. Ancient Peruvian
33. Bronx cheer
36. Roswell crash victim, supposedly
38. Last name in fashion
39. Besmirch
40. Able to see right through
41. Expectorated matter
43. As a result
45. Rimsky-Korsakov's "The Tale of ___ Saltan"
46. Pseudonym
48. Inflammation
50. ___ terrier
51. Consequently
53. Affranchise
56. "Get it?"
58. Simon Legree
60. Bother
61. Noted blind mathematician
64. Bride
66. Composed
67. Part of N.Y.C.
68. Donations
69. Tolkien creatures
70. "Wheel of Fortune" purchase
71. Contents of some bags

Down

1. Want to
2. Vinyl collectible
3. Hit the slopes
4. Newspaper section
5. Clean up, in a way
6. Gives a hand
7. "___ the season ..."
8. Aardvark's morsel
9. A nonconformist person
10. Kind of court
11. Vexes
12. Name holder
14. Alkaline liquid
16. Reverse, e.g.
20. Calypso offshoot
25. Pilot's announcement, briefly
26. Driver in flight
27. Hungarian composer and pianist
28. Shipping hazard
29. "La Scala di ___" (Rossini opera)
30. Fingers
31. Australasian nipa palm
32. Camp
34. Bookkeeping entry
35. Measure
37. ___'easter
42. "___ questions?"
44. For all to see
47. "Is it soup ___?"
49. "Do ___ others..."
51. Coach
52. Half of Hispaniola
53. Big dipper
54. Tomato blight
55. High spots
56. Darn
57. Coin with 12 stars on it
59. Pool site, maybe
62. And so on
63. ___ judicata
65. Blackguard

PUZZLE 42

Across
1. Hog haven
4. Attention
8. Aforementioned
12. ___ gin fizz
13. Big production
14. Kind of drive
16. Em, to Dorothy
17. Bass
18. Kind of layer
19. Beer bust essential
20. Careless
21. Mouth, slangily
23. Bottom line
24. Any Time
26. Finish (up)
28. Anatomical pouch
30. Coxcomb
32. Blockheads
36. "Oh, ___!"
39. A bit cracked
41. Get away
42. "Act your ___!"
43. Colorful parrot
45. Detergent brand
46. Beef cut
48. Sandwich shop
49. Many elms
50. Goatish glance
51. Band performance
52. Jewel
54. "That means ___!"
56. Continental money
60. Adept
63. "Go on"
65. Come together
67. Order between "ready" and "fire"
68. Emotion
70. Call
72. Game piece
73. Excuse
74. "Iliad" warrior
75. Hasenpfeffer, e.g.
76. Priestly garb
77. Its motto is "Lux et veritas"
78. Cushion

Down
1. Swings around
2. Hammer's partner
3. At a future time
4. End piece
5. Crown
6. Bemoan
7. Make out
8. Check (out)
9. Cutting tool
10. Caddie's offering
11. Exhausted, with "in"
12. Pseudonym of H. H. Munro
15. Assembled
20. Grazing spot
22. Cleo's undoing
25. Can. neighbor
27. Distress
29. Video maker, for short
30. Aspect
31. Kind of hygiene
33. Figure skater's jump
34. Al dente
35. "Don't go!"
36. Fertilizer
37. Chill
38. Same: Fr.
40. Green gem
44. Top secret?
47. Jimmy
49. Low-fat meat
51. Juliet, to Romeo
53. Electric fish
55. Desert sight
57. Yogurt and cucumber dish
58. Blotto
59. Old World duck
60. ___ king
61. Pepsi, for one
62. Blackhearted
64. 6/6/44
65. Highlander
66. "If all ___ fails..."
69. Drop
71. Grp. involved in "the Troubles"
72. Medicinal amt.

PUZZLE 43

Across
1. Battle of Britain grp.
4. Priests' vestments
8. Egg
12. Maui dance
13. Sack
14. CeO2
16. Any day now
17. Eye up and down
18. Ever
19. Neighbor of Fiji
21. Enter eagerly
23. Hoof sound
24. Chemical suffix
25. Bent
27. "That feels good!"
29. Grab (onto)
30. "___ Miniver"
31. Bounce
34. Mother of Elizabeth I
37. "One of ___" (Willa Cather novel)
38. Aloof
39. Track
40. Append
41. Winston Churchill's "___ Country"
42. Baseball's Mel
43. Come down
45. Bag
47. "___ Loves You"
48. Boundary
49. Perry Como's "___ Loves Mambo"
50. Expected
51. Feed bag contents
52. TV monitor?
55. ___-European
58. Cordial
60. Dig
62. Cousin of a raccoon
64. Australasian nipa palm
66. Circus cries
67. "Come in!"
68. Blue shade
69. Small cave
70. Comfort
71. "Or ___!"
72. Catullus composition

Down
1. Chatter
2. "Home ___"
3. Tooth
4. Blood-typing system
5. Deadlock
6. Veterinary medicine
7. Flower holder
8. Wood sorrel
9. Climbing plant
10. Caspian feeder
11. Actor O'Shea
12. Abhor
15. Mont Blanc, e.g.
20. Well
22. Henry VIII's last wife
26. H+, e.g.
28. Bubblehead
29. Do goo
30. Kind of pie
31. LP player
32. Wood sorrels
33. Combustible heap
34. Boys in the 'hood
35. "@#$%!," e.g.
36. Dietary, in ads
37. Kooky
40. "Go on..."
41. ___ maison (indoors): Fr.
43. Money in Moldova
44. Avon anti-aging brand
45. Port vessel
46. Basilica area
49. Argentine grassland
50. Shower with love
51. Cantilevered window
52. Greenland sight
53. Small salmon
54. Dermatologist's concern
55. Crystal meth, in slang
56. ___ the wiser
57. Computer info
59. Add to the pot
61. Inoperative
63. Dander
65. Bass, for one

PUZZLE 44

Across

1. Mins. and mins.
4. Pop-ups, e.g.
7. Waves
11. Gunk
12. Norse goddess of fate
13. "He's ___ nowhere man" (Beatles lyric)
15. Downtown
17. Provide, as with a quality
18. Botheration
19. Power problem
21. Kind of fingerprint
22. Bumped into
23. Abdicator of 1917
24. Poor, as excuses go
27. Course requirement?
28. Enclose
30. On a deck, perhaps
33. Assert
36. Architectural projection
38. About noon
39. Hail, to Caesar
40. Hit, in a way
41. British author of historical novels
43. Enrich, in a way
45. ___ fruit
46. Partner
48. PC program
50. Brain section
51. Betting game
53. "Catch-22" pilot
56. Diamond stat
58. State of affairs
60. Kind of patch
61. Void
64. For sin
66. The end
67. Double-decker checker
68. Used as fertilizer
69. Lodge
70. Compass dir.
71. Big mouth

Down

1. Crush
2. Automaton
3. Bathroom installation
4. Blood line
5. Gloomy, in poetry
6. Fly in the ointment
7. Freelancer's enc.
8. Coffee ___
9. Shame
10. Italian diety
11. Marianas island
12. Sartre novel
14. Meadow
16. Do, say
20. "Slippery" tree
25. ___ system
26. Increase
27. Kind of artist
28. Decorative pitcher
29. Fall (over)
30. Chucklehead
31. Jiffs
32. Orbiting a star
34. Caesar's farewell
35. Female gametes
37. Island chain
42. Butter holder
44. Risk
47. Yellow, for one
49. Ask
51. Belong
52. Agreeing (with)
53. "Lohengrin," e.g.
54. Extend, in a way
55. Pro follower
56. Old name for Tokyo
57. Edges
59. Benefit
62. Before now
63. Crude
65. Closemouthed

PUZZLE 45

Across

1. A Hindu sage
6. Lyndon Johnson dog
9. Unwanted e-mail
13. Colorado resort
14. Fertility clinic stock
15. Ancient city NW of Carthage
16. Luxurious
17. It's catching
18. Month after Adar
19. Passion
21. Oil-rich land
23. Low-fat meat source
24. Copter's forerunner
25. Appropriate
28. Donald and Ivana, e.g.
30. Body
35. Accommodate
37. A fan of
39. Bake
40. Consequently
41. Needle point?
43. Caribbean and others
44. Beautify
46. For dieters
47. ___ noir
48. Catholic diplomat
50. Cliff's pal on "Cheers"
52. Gloomy
53. Noise made by an engine
55. Bit in a horse's mouth
57. Look down on with disdain
61. Really good
65. In conflict with, with "of"
66. + or - item
68. Mark
69. Wet, weatherwise
70. Double standard?
71. Basket material
72. Combustible pile
73. Dark time for poets
74. Perfect, e.g.

Down

1. Criticizes
2. Catalina, e.g.
3. Spin
4. "Siddhartha" author
5. Bury
6. Wolf's sound
7. Twelfth Night, vis-à-vis Epiphany
8. Browning's Ben Ezra, e.g.
9. Awaken
10. Galileo's birthplace
11. Small dark purple fruit
12. "Buddenbrooks" author
15. After catching
20. A plant hormone
22. Parenthesis, essentially
24. Woman's clothing piece, small
25. Associated with terrorism
26. Concealed
27. Append
29. Chemical compound
31. A kind of computer architecture
32. Beg
33. Muddle
34. City in North Rhine-Westphalia
36. Rigid necklace
38. "Beetle Bailey" pooch
42. Great white ___
45. O.K.
49. Eponymous physicist
51. Larva
54. Bond
56. Breviloquent
57. Be a kvetch
58. (usually derogatory) a white person
59. Film ___
60. Ditty
61. Any minute
62. Been in bed
63. Day of the month
64. Waxy covering, birds
67. Be in arrears

PUZZLE 46

Across
1. Make tracks?
4. Bake sale org.
7. Bindle bearer
11. Double
12. Poet
13. Lifeless
15. Overuse
17. Jiltee of myth
18. "Shoot!"
19. "Potemkin" setting
21. Sly
22. "___ me?"
23. Long jaw fish
24. Ear part
27. "Yeah, ___!"
28. Bar order
30. Man, for one
33. Honey
36. A thin layer or stratum of rock
38. Earth
39. Boy
40. Pound, e.g.
41. Sugar ___
43. 10 C-notes
45. Swim
46. "Now!"
48. "Whew!"
50. It has a big mouth
51. ___ Mix
53. ___ de Triomphe
56. Fancy neckwear
58. Cultivated his own land
60. Open tract
61. Below
64. Horizontal plant stem
66. Cordwood measure
67. ___ of the Apostles
68. Loafer, e.g.
69. Assayers' stuff
70. "Ain't ___ Sweet"
71. Calphalon product

Down
1. Swagger
2. Lively, exciting, thrilling
3. Publicity, slangily
4. Pay money
5. Amount of hair
6. Annexes
7. "It Must Be ___"
8. "Take ___"
9. Temporary associate
10. ___ O's (Post cereal)
11. Become friendlier
12. Smear
14. Burden
16. NASA scrub
20. Sierra Nevada, e.g.
25. Amiss
26. Disease?
27. Chicken
28. Completely fix
29. Place
30. Belief system
31. "General Hospital," e.g.
32. See the spoken word
34. Choir part
35. "Phooey!"
37. 20's dispenser
42. Compass heading
44. Depth charge targets
47. "Don't give up!"
49. Admits, with "up"
51. Bum
52. Be theatrical
53. Football's ___ Bowl
54. Scout's mission
55. Harden
56. Greyhound, e.g.
57. Aware of
59. Big times
62. Bard's "before"
63. ___ publica
65. Recipe amt.

PUZZLE 47

Across

1. Ed.'s request
4. Experienced
8. Back talk
12. Icy
13. Claudius's successor
14. Destroyer destroyer
16. "For ___ us a child is born ..."
17. Pitcher
18. Dangerous bacteria
19. "Go team!"
20. Collector's goal
21. Doze
23. Bring home
24. Tolerate
26. Island chain?
28. ___ Master's Voice
30. Free from, with "of"
32. Brazil, Paraguay, language
36. Plant stem of Gramineae
39. Exuberance
41. Spin
42. Earlier
43. Attractive woman
45. Frequently, in poetry
46. Concrete section
48. Turkish leader
49. Data
50. LP player
51. "The loneliest number"
52. "Amen!"
54. Feathered stole
56. Copious
60. Clever
63. Crack, so to speak
65. Choose
67. "We've been ___!"
68. See the info
70. Choir voice
72. God
73. À la King
74. Milldam
75. It's a sin
76. Equal
77. Adam's apple spot
78. Darjeeling or oolong

Down

1. Navigational aid
2. Even if, briefly
3. Old Tokyo
4. Cap site
5. Colorful salamander
6. Before, before
7. Dog-eared
8. Glove material
9. "Poison Arrow" band
10. Sometime today, say
11. After-Christmas event
12. Rein in
15. Small songbird
20. Schuss
22. Ancient
25. Its symbol is an omega
27. "___ time"
29. Make a seam
30. Cooktop
31. Narrow margin
33. ___ reflection
34. Magic Dragon
35. Absorbed by
36. Bills, e.g.
37. Wrinkly fruit
38. Do nothing
40. Economical
44. Cow chow
47. Chest protector
49. Doctrine
51. Blade
53. Absorb, as a cost
55. Catchall category
57. Call
58. Grub
59. Christian Science founder
60. Gray, in a way
61. Get ready, for short
62. Container weight
64. Open wide
65. Auditory
66. Bacon
69. ___-eyed
71. "Malcolm X" director
72. Allow

PUZZLE 48

Across

1. Slips
7. Blond shade
10. Buddy
14. Deli order
15. Island strings
16. Delicate
17. 2-Years to grad
20. Flower part
21. La lead-in
22. Stage item
23. Dugout, for one
26. Compass reading
28. Day ___
31. Privileged
37. Play boisterously
39. Flat bread
40. Atlas section
41. Criticize harshly
42. Mass of flocculent material
43. Pull-off
46. Coarse and contemptible in behaviour
48. Dismiss
50. Congeal
51. Hooter
52. Explode
54. Ban
58. Word with bum or bunny
60. One with notions
64. Focus on the little things
68. In the center of
69. Altar vow
70. Supporting Islam
71. Decomposes
72. Drops on blades
73. Burn

Down

1. Extended periods
2. Medical advice, often
3. Con
4. Enormous energy
5. Dick
6. "Wheel of Fortune" request
7. Mercury, for one
8. Halloween costume
9. Common contraction
10. Star followers
11. Affectation
12. Arborist's concern
13. Observer
18. ___ spumante
19. Build
24. Crew member
25. Dance, e.g.
27. ___'wester
28. Line of cliffs
29. Leisurely walk
30. Dispatch boat
32. Kind of infection
33. Jazz bit
34. "___ well"
35. Intimate
36. Marina sight
38. Curse
41. On the side
44. Ribbon holder
45. Haul
46. A Beatle bride
47. Give it ___
49. Bibliographical abbr.
53. Bright circle?
54. Autocrat
55. BBs, e.g.
56. Can of worms?
57. Cutlass, e.g.
59. Comprehend
61. Blab
62. Employed
63. Schools of thought
65. Prefix with night or day
66. German resort
67. Med school grad

PUZZLE 49

1	2	3	4	5	6		7	8	9		10	11	12	13
14							15				16			
17					18				19					
20					21				22					
		23	24	25			26	27						
28	29	30		31		32				33	34	35	36	
37			38			39								
40				41					42					
43			44	45				46	47					
48						49				50				
		51				52		53						
54	55	56	57			58	59			60	61	62	63	
64				65			66	67						
68				69			70							
71				72			73							

Across

1. J. Edgar Hoover's org.
4. Memory unit
8. Big name in mapmaking
12. All ___
13. Animal house?
14. Not silently
16. Marianas island
17. Cemetery sights
18. European capital
19. Bic filler
20. Bloodshot
21. Dwindle
23. Checkers, e.g.
24. Approval
26. Furnace fuel
28. Island ring
30. When repeated, a dance
32. Beast
36. Kind of child
39. Money in Western Samoa
41. Like Superman's vision
42. "A pox on you!"
43. La ___
45. It needs refinement
46. Sped
48. LP player
49. Awfully long time
50. Antitoxins
51. High school class
52. Court ploy
54. Brace
56. No longer in
60. Mock, in a way
63. Hog heaven?
65. Heel
67. It's cut and dried
68. Irish word for a lake
70. Cobblers' tools
72. Hawk's opposite
73. Endured
74. "Groovy!"
75. Burns up
76. 2:00 or 3:00
77. Apteryx australis
78. Coast Guard rank: Abbr.

Down

1. It's a part of life
2. Covered with undergrowth
3. Doctrine: Suffix
4. Bummed out
5. Place to play
6. Bolivian export
7. Gaelic
8. Browning's Ben Ezra, e.g.
9. Bar order
10. Average guy?
11. Buggy terrain
12. Protection: Var.
15. Cave
20. Beluga yield
22. Feathery wrap
25. Artful
27. Nova, e.g.
29. "___ true!"
30. Allegation
31. Fair share, maybe
33. Hot drink
34. Pink, as a steak
35. "___ only"
36. Ices
37. "Cleopatra" backdrop
38. Lascivious look
40. Sore
44. Be bedridden
47. Roll of bills
49. Grp. concerned with defense
51. Contracted
53. Like some socks
55. One who puts you in your place
57. Pricker
58. Overhangs
59. Colors
60. Priest's robe
61. "Fiddlesticks!"
62. Continental capital
64. A-Rod, for one
65. Manhandle
66. Italian province or its capital
69. Bearded beast
71. Many Chinese dynasty
72. Fizzle out

PUZZLE 50

	1	2	3		4	5	6	7		8	9	10	11	
12					13					14				15
16					17					18				
19				20				21	22			23		
24			25						26		27			
			28		29		30	31			32	33	34	35
36	37	38			39	40				41				
42					43			44			45			
46			47		48					49				
50				51			52	53						
			54	55					56		57	58	59	
60	61	62		63		64		65	66		67			
68			69			70	71			72				
73					74					75				
	76				77					78				

103

PUZZLE 1

A	S	S	A	M		A	B	E	T		W	H	I	P
S	O	L	F	A		S	E	A	S		A	I	N	U
P	L	U	T	O		E	A	G	E	R	N	E	S	S
S	O	M	E	R	S	A	U	L	T	E	D			
	S	P	R	I	T			E	S	P		B	A	G
		T	S	A	R	S		E	O	C	E	N	E	
A	Q	U	A		R	O	O	D		T	A	L	O	N
N	U	N	S		R	E	L	I	C		R	A	L	E
G	A	I	T	S		S	A	S	H		B	Y	E	S
E	S	T	E	E	M		R	H	I	N	O			
L	I	E		N	U	B		L	I	N	A	C		
		U	S	E	R	F	R	I	E	N	D	L	Y	
W	H	O	L	E	S	A	L	E		C	A	M	E	O
Y	A	W	N		L	I	E	F		E	D	I	F	Y
E	T	N	A		I	D	E	S		S	E	T	T	O

PUZZLE 2

A	L	T	O		T	E	S	T		S	C	E	N	E
M	I	R	V		E	G	O	S		T	A	P	E	R
B	R	E	A	C	H	O	F	P	R	O	M	I	S	E
O	A	K		A	R	I	A		E	R	E	C	T	
			S	P	A	S		A	C	E	R			
A	C	C	O	U	N	T	S	P	A	Y	A	B	L	E
S	A	U	L	T			A	S	P	S		L	E	A
P	I	P	E			R	Y	E			L	A	W	S
I	R	E		E	G	I	S			A	E	R	I	E
C	O	L	D	B	L	O	O	D	E	D	N	E	S	S
			A	B	E	T		E	N	I	D			
Y	E	N	T	A		A	M	M	O			F	D	A
L	E	A	D	I	N	G	Q	U	E	S	T	I	O	N
E	A	S	E	D			O	U	R	S		U	N	T	O
T	H	E	R	E		D	A	S	H		B	E	E	N

PUZZLE 3

	S	A	C	K	B	U	T		S	W	A	G	S	
I	N	C	H	O	A	T	E		W	H	I	L	E	D
C	O	N	O	I	D	A	L		A	I	R	I	E	R
E	W	E	R		H	E	F	T	S		T	R	Y	
			E	S	T		P	A	C	K	E	T		
A	L	P	A	C	A		H	U	H		T	E	A	K
D	A	H		A	P	R	O	N		A	A	R	G	H
O	B	I		M	A	E	N	A	D	S		A	R	M
P	O	L	Y	P		T	E	E	U	P		T	E	E
T	R	I	O		M	A	N		M	E	T	I	E	R
		S	U	D	O	K	U		B	R	O			
O	F	T		E	D	E	M	A		O	D	D	S	
T	R	I	S	T	E		B	U	R	N	T	O	U	T
T	A	N	K	E	R		E	T	I	O	L	O	G	Y
	Y	E	A	R	N		R	O	B	B	E	R	S	

PUZZLE 4

T	O	D	D		H	A	V	O	C		A	D	D	S
A	G	U	E		A	M	I	N	O		R	O	O	T
G	E	M	S		C	O	M	E	D	I	E	N	N	E
S	E	P	P	U	K	U	S			D	A	U	N	T
			O	P	E	N		C	U	E	S	T	A	S
D	I	S	T	O	R	T	I	O	N	S				
U	N	P	I	N			S	L	I	T		S	A	P
O	T	I	C		S	P	L	A	T		C	O	M	E
S	O	T		D	E	L	E			E	O	S	I	N
			W	E	A	T	H	E	R	W	O	R	N	
C	O	N	T	E	M	N		I	N	N	S			
A	W	A	R	E		G	A	Z	E	L	L	E	S	
R	I	S	I	B	I	L	I	T	Y		I	O	T	A
G	N	A	T		S	E	R	U	M		P	O	U	R
O	G	L	E		M	O	O	S	E		S	K	I	D

PUZZLE 5

H	E	A	P		S	L	A	G		A	B	A	S	E
A	M	B	O		C	O	L	A		B	O	S	K	S
D	U	A	L	C	I	T	I	Z	E	N	S	H	I	P
			T	O	O	T		A	N	O	N			
L	A	D	R	O	N	E		T	R	I	A	L	S	
O	D	E	O	N	S		E	G	O	M	A	N	I	A
P	O	C	O		K	A	R	M	A		O	D	D	
		I	N	T	A	N	G	I	B	L	E	S		
I	S	M		A	C	O	R	N		X	M	A	S	
D	E	A	F	M	U	T	E		S	P	L	I	C	E
S	A	L	A	A	M		S	T	R	I	A	T	E	
		U	R	E	A		C	R	I	B				
E	V	E	N	I	N	G	P	R	I	M	R	O	S	E
V	E	G	A	N		A	R	I	A		I	D	E	S
E	G	G	E	D		R	O	P	E		S	E	T	T

PUZZLE 6

T	W	A	S		E	B	B	E	D		S	N	O	T
R	I	C	H		D	E	I	T	Y		W	I	L	E
E	R	N	E		U	L	N	A	E		I	S	L	E
K	E	E	L		C	O	O		G	R	E	A	T	
			F	R	E	N	C	H	P	O	L	I	S	H
P	A	U	L	I		G	U	A	R	D				
A	U	R	I	G	A		L	I	E		R	Y	E	S
T	R	A	F	A	L	G	A	R	S	Q	U	A	R	E
H	A	L	E		T	O	R		S	U	M	M	I	T
				S	H	A	V	E		A	P	S	E	S
H	A	L	F	H	O	L	I	D	A	Y	S			
I	N	U	R	E		S	I	M		T	A	M	P	
K	O	T	O		B	R	I	B	E		E	N	O	L
E	D	E	N		A	N	O	L	E		A	O	N	E
R	E	S	T		S	A	N	E	R		K	N	O	B

PUZZLE 7

P	A	S	T		T	A	B	S		V	I	O	L	A
A	L	E	E		O	K	R	A		E	M	A	I	L
N	A	P	E		R	I	A	L		R	A	T	E	L
D	R	I	N	K	I	N	G	S	O	N	G			
A	M	A	T	I		A	V	A	I	L	E	D		
			S	T	E	A	L		A	L	S	A	C	E
P	R	A	Y	E	R	F	U	L		M	U	L	E	
E	O	N		D	R	A	G	O	O	N		G	A	M
A	V	I	D		R	E	D	L	I	G	H	T	S	
R	E	M	I	N	D		S	E	D	E	R			
T	R	A	V	O	I	S		C	A	R	T	S		
		O	N	E	H	O	R	S	E	T	O	W	N	
W	H	A	R	F		A	N	O	A		I	D	E	A
E	R	I	C	A		R	U	I	N		F	E	A	R
I	S	L	E	T		I	S	L	E		Y	O	K	E

PUZZLE 8

R	A	G		E	A	T	S		L	H	A	S	A
A	C	E		A	L	E	E		P	O	I	S	O	N
G	E	N	E	R	A	L	E	L	E	C	T	I	O	N
G	R	O	A	T	S		P	A	R	A		A	N	A
A	B	A	S	H		O	S	C	U	L	E			
			T	S	A	R			A	G	A	P	E	
A	B	A		H	I	E	D		E	N	A	M	O	R
C	O	C	K	A	D	O	O	D	L	E	D	O	O	S
T	R	A	I	T	S		C	U	S	S		S	H	E
S	T	I	N	T		S	E	T	S					
			D	E	S	E	R	T		H	O	U	R	I
E	R	A		R	O	V	E		B	E	A	R	E	R
C	O	N	F	I	D	E	N	C	E	T	R	I	C	K
R	E	T	I	N	A		T	O	R	I		A	T	E
U	S	I	N	G		S	Y	N	C		H	O	D	

PUZZLE 9

PUZZLE 10

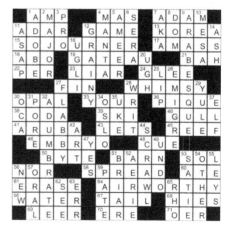

PUZZLE 11

PUZZLE 12

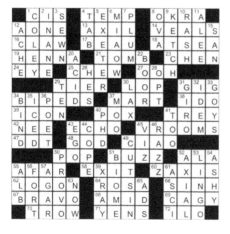

PUZZLE 13

1 P	2 I	3 T	4 T	5 A		6 U	7 L	8 T			9 G	10 H	11 E	12 E
13 A	M	O	U	R		14 N	E	E		15 S	A	U	R	Y
16 G	A	M	B	A		17 T	A	M		18 E	E	R	I	E
19 E	M	B	A	R	20 G	O		21 P	22 S	A	L	T	E	R
			23 L	A	Y		24 T	O	A	D				
25 A	26 L	27 L		28 T	R	29 E	E		30 C	O	31 M	32 M	33 A	34 S
35 L	E	A	36 F		37 O	L	L	38 A		39 G	U	I	R	O
40 T	O	P	I		41 S	A	L	O	42 N		43 T	A	E	L
44 A	N	E	N	45 T		46 N	I	N	E		47 T	O	N	E
48 R	E	L	O	A	49 D		50 N	E	E	51 D		52 W	A	D
				53 R	U	54 N	G		55 D	U	56 E			
57 B	58 R	59 Y	60 O	Z	O	A		61 P	Y	R	A	62 M	63 I	64 D
65 Y	A	L	T	A		66 T	67 O	O		68 E	R	O	D	E
69 T	I	E	I	N		70 C	A	D		71 S	T	I	L	E
72 E	L	M	S			73 H	R	S		74 S	H	L	E	P

PUZZLE 14

1 C	2 E	3 L	4 E	5 B		6 H	7 A	8 W	9 S		10 E	11 T	12 C	13 H
14 O	P	I	N	E		15 A	G	R	A		16 T	H	E	E
17 L	E	A	C	H		18 S	H	U	L		19 C	R	A	W
20 T	E	R	R	A	21 S		22 A	N	A	23 L		24 U	S	E
			25 Y	L	E	26 M		27 G	R	O	28 O	M	E	D
29 L	30 E	31 A	P	F	R	O	32 G		33 Y	A	W			
34 E	X	I	T		35 B	L	O	36 C		37 D	E	38 U	39 C	40 E
41 G	A	D			42 S	T	Y	L	43 I			44 R	O	D
45 O	M	E	46 G	47 A		48 S	I	A	N		49 U	G	L	I
			50 E	B	51 B		52 M	I	S	53 T	R	E	A	T
54 F	55 O	56 R	M	U	L	57 A		58 M	E	S	A			
59 A	L	E		60 T	A	L	61 L		62 T	E	N	63 P	64 I	65 N
66 I	D	E	67 S		68 N	O	E	69 L		70 T	I	A	R	A
71 N	I	L	E		72 C	H	O	U		73 S	U	G	A	R
74 T	E	S	T		75 H	A	N	G		76 E	M	E	N	D

PUZZLE 15

1 N	2 A	3 A	4 N		5 A	6 D	7 A	8 M			9 S	10 P	11 A	12 T
13 E	N	C	O	14 U	R	A	G	E	15 D		16 E	I	R	E
17 D	E	M	O	N	O	L	O	G	Y		18 A	C	R	E
	19 W	E	N	D	S		20 G	O	N	21 G		22 C	O	N
			23 D	I	E	24 T		25 H	E	E	26 H	A	W	
27 S	28 T	29 E	A	D		30 H	31 I	M		32 E	E	L		
33 A	R	M	Y		34 N	A	G		35 A	U	R	I	36 G	37 A
38 N	I	B		39 B	U	I	L	40 T	U	P		41 L	A	W
42 S	O	R	43 B	E	T		44 O	A	K		45 O	L	I	O
		46 O	A	F		47 L	O	P		48 A	X	I	A	L
	49 M	I	M	O	S	50 A		51 A	52 S	C	I			
53 B	E	D		54 G	U	R	55 U		56 N	I	D	57 U	58 S	
59 A	D	E	60 N		61 D	I	S	62 S	O	N	A	N	C	63 E
64 S	I	R	E		65 S	A	S	H	W	I	N	D	O	W
66 K	A	Y	O			67 T	R	E	Y		68 T	O	T	E

PUZZLE 16

1 A	2 P	3 E	4 R		5 S	6 A	7 Y	8 S		9 E	10 L	11 G	12 A	13 R
14 T	A	X	I		15 O	S	L	O		16 V	E	R	S	O
17 S	U	P	S		18 I	C	E	D		19 E	V	I	C	T
20 E	L	E	C	21 T	R	O	M	A	22 G	N	E	T	I	C
23 A	I	L		24 R	E	T			25 U	S	E			
			26 T	E	E		27 F	28 I	L	O		29 D	30 I	31 P
32 A	33 G	34 O	R	A		35 I	O	T	A		36 T	O	D	O
37 V	E	G	E	T	38 A	B	L	E	G	39 A	R	D	E	N
40 O	N	L	Y		41 H	E	L	M		42 L	O	O	S	E
43 W	E	E		44 F	O	X	Y		45 S	O	T			
			46 O	I	L			47 O	N	O		48 P	49 A	50 S
51 A	52 T	53 T	H	E	D	54 R	55 O	P	O	F	56 A	H	A	T
57 L	O	A	M	S		58 A	L	A	R		59 B	O	R	A
60 U	N	L	I	T		61 S	I	R	E		62 E	N	O	L
63 M	E	C	C	A		64 P	O	T	S		65 D	Y	N	E

PUZZLE 17

H	E	R	A	L	D		O	P	T		S	C	A	M
E	L	I	D	E	D		P	A	W		O	R	S	O
A	S	A	M	A	T	T	E	R	O	F	F	A	C	T
D	E	L	I			A	C	T		R	A	M	I	E
			T	A	E	L		I	O	U				
P	A	P		D	R	E	S	S	C	I	R	C	L	E
O	R	A	T	O	R		T	A	T	T	E	R	E	D
S	E	R	A		T	O	N			L	O	G	E	
S	N	A	C	K	B	A	R		P	A	Y	N	I	M
E	A	S	T	E	R	N	M	O	S	T		E	T	A
			B	A	D		P	I	E	D				
A	T	S	E	A		O	R	E		A	N	T	E	
C	O	L	D	B	L	O	O	D	E	D	N	E	S	S
E	T	U	I		E	R	A		S	A	T	R	A	P
D	E	B	T		G	I	N		T	H	E	O	R	Y

PUZZLE 18

A	U	R	A		S	T	E	E	P		A	C	H	E
P	R	O	W		A	W	A	K	E		T	H	U	D
S	A	I	N	T	P	E	T	E	R	S	B	U	R	G
E	L	L		A	P	E	S		E	A	G	L	E	
			E	C	H	T		B	O	X	Y			
S	T	I	N	K	O		B	E	A	U		O	P	S
P	O	N	D		K	A	S	H	A		P	E	E	
R	U	S	S	I	A	N	R	O	U	L	E	T	T	E
E	R	E		S	N	O	O	T		M	E	A	D	
E	S	T		S	O	W	N		A	V	I	D	L	Y
		Y	U	A	N		A	L	I	T				
S	E	T	A	E		I	R	I	S		L	E	U	
P	R	O	C	R	A	S	T	I	N	A	T	I	N	G
A	N	K	H		G	E	E	S	E		E	V	I	L
M	E	E	T		A	C	M	E	S		C	E	D	I

PUZZLE 19

E	C	L	A	T		O	R	A	L		A	R	I	A
T	H	E	S	E		M	A	N	A		N	A	R	C
H	I	G	H	E	R	E	D	U	C	A	T	I	O	N
O	R	G	Y		E	G	I	S		B	E	N	N	E
S	P	Y		C	I	A	O		R	I	S	C		
			C	O	N		T	H	A	T		H	E	R
O	V	O	L	O		A	E	O	N		L	E	V	I
R	I	B	O	N	U	C	L	E	I	C	A	C	I	D
F	I	S	T		S	H	E	S		A	N	K	L	E
F	I	T		L	E	Y	S		L	S	D			
		R	A	I	D		C	R	E	E		F	L	U
O	V	U	L	E		B	O	O	N		E	L	A	N
P	I	C	T	U	R	E	P	O	S	T	C	A	R	D
A	L	T	O		A	Y	E	S		S	H	I	V	E
L	E	S	S		P	S	S	T		P	O	L	A	R

PUZZLE 20

A	V	E	S		M	O	W		B	A	I	L
L	I	R	A		B	A	R	E		C	I	R	C	A
A	L	I	T		U	N	I	T		R	O	C	K	Y
R	E	E	N	T	R	I	E	S		A	S	H	Y	
			A	R	E	A	L		E	T	C			
T	R	I	V	I	A		A	R	E	O	L	A	R
E	E	L		M	U	R	M	U	R		P	A	C	E
S	L	I	T	S		O	I	L		G	E	N	R	E
L	I	A	R		R	I	D	D	L	E		A	I	D
A	C	C	U	S	A	L		U	N	T	I	D	Y
			E	L	F		D	E	M	U	R			
H	A	L	O		B	O	M	B	S	I	G	H	T
A	E	S	O	P		L	U	B	E		U	R	E	A
C	R	A	V	E		U	S	E	R		N	A	R	C
T	O	P	E		R	E	D		E	D	D	O

PUZZLE 21

```
T O M B   S A C R A     R A G S
A R I A   A G L E T   I N O N
P A N T Y W A I S T   S T O A
E L I T E   P I E R C I N G
        T A I   G N U
    D R I B S A N D D R A B S
P E R I   E L D   D E C A L
A R I D   D E I T Y   L U L U
P I L O T   E Y E   I T E M
S E L F A S S U R A N C E
        C P U   O R E
N E W W O R L D   A L L O T
A C R E   U P R O A R I O U S
S H I N   C H E E P   R O S A
H O T S   E A G R E   A P E R
```

PUZZLE 22

```
S P A N     S L O B   O G L E
T U L I P   H O P E   P L E A
A R E N A   R O A R   T A P S
G R E A T N E P H E W   S T Y
        S O D   F A T W A
S A T Y R   R E T I R E
P U M A   T O O K   F A G O T
T E A K   H O V E R   N I G H
A D L I B   P E S O   C A R E
    G N E I S S   S C E N E
R A G A S   H I E
G A M   R A N K A N D F I L E
A G A R   I O N S   A L D E R
Z E T A   A T O P   R I L E S
E D E N   H E W S   T Y K E
```

PUZZLE 23

```
O P U S   W A D E     A D O
L U G E   E L I T E   A V I D
I S L E   A L O U D   S E E D
V A I N G L O R I O U S
E N S   E T C   S E E D S
    R E H A B   E A T O U T
A L I A S   T E A R   S E A
C E N T E R O F G R A V I T Y
I M F   P R I G   L I N O S
D O R S U M   T R A L A
S N A P S   A P E   O I L
    R E C O N V E Y A N C E
S A K I   I B E A M   C A I N
T W I G   A O R T A   H I N T
Y E N     E D E N   E R G O
```

PUZZLE 24

```
A P S E   S E V E R   A M O S
B R A D   U N I T E   N A P E
C O K E   M A I N E   S C A N
    F I N A N C I A L Y E A R S
        W E T   E L U T E
T R A C E R   M A D A M
B E T A   M E M O S   E S T
S T O R E D E T E C T I V E S
P E P   R E R A N   L I R A
    L A B E L   C A L L E R
A S S E T   H O D
D I A M O N D W E D D I N G
O N T O   O R I N G   N E O N
P A I N   D A N C E   C R E E
T I N Y   S T E E R   H O S T
```

PUZZLE 25

```
C R A M   C I R C E   B O N E
L O T I   O C E A N   O B E Y
A D O S   C O N I C   L O R E
S E L F C O N T R O L L E D
P O L I O       O R E
    T R I A L   E K E O U T
O D E   A T R I A   A N N E
V I T A L S T A T I S T I C S
E R A S   S N O R E   T O T
N E L S O N   A M E B A
    P E N     U M B R A
    F A I T S A C C O M P L I S
F E U D   T R O O P   E E L S
E A R L   L E O N E   R A L E
B R A E   E S S E N   E R S T
```

PUZZLE 26

```
T I P   R A D A R   M A D A M
R N A   A B A C A   A L I B I
I C E   Y A C H T   N O M A D
B I L L O F H E A L T H
A T L A N T A     L A A G E R
L E A R   S O F A   S A M E
      V E G   M I N D   S U V
    C A N I N E T O O T H
E G O   D R A G   S E W
G E R M   D Y A D   I C E S
G E N I A L   E M A N A T E
      D U E D I L I G E N C E
E M B A R   E D E M A   O H M
M A R I A   A L T E R   E E L
S N A R L   N E E D S   D R Y
```

PUZZLE 27

```
M I L L   S P E C   S T U F F
A N O A   E A C H   M A N I A
N E T T   A G H A   E X I S T
A R T I C L E O F F A I T H
S T E N O   E A R
    A R D O R   A S L E E P
T A B   G O R E D   E R R S
A M E R I C A N I N D I A N S
P E R I   L A N A I   S E T
A N G O R A   L E G A L
    I T S   R I C K S
    S E L F E M P L O Y M E N T
N O P A L   A R I A   P L E A
E L I T E   C A R S   I L L S
D I C E R   K Y A T   D O T H
```

PUZZLE 28

```
S T O W   G O T H   L O P E
A R G O   O U S E   F I L E R
M A R K E T G A R D E N I N G
E Y E   B O H R   E N D O N
      B U T   W A D E
W Y A T T   A I R   N I N A
H O U R I   P I G M Y   D O C
A R M E D T O T H E T E E T H
I S M   E R E C T   T R A C E
L E Y S   A S H   F R E S H
    A D D Y   L E I
G E N I E   L I E U   U S A
B A C K G R O U N D M U S I C
A P H I S   O G E E   F E L T
N E O N   H E R R   O D D S
```

PUZZLE 29

S	C	R	A	P		T	W	A	S		G	N	U	S
O	M	A	N	I		H	A	S	P		R	I	N	K
M	O	N	T	E		R	I	C	E		A	S	I	A
A	N	T	I	B	I	O	T	I	C		N	E	A	T
			A	V	E			I	G	N	I	T	E	
S	L	O	W	L	Y		P	O	E	S	Y			
L	I	V	I	D		R	H	O		A	K	R	O	N
O	M	A	N		O	O	H		N	A	M	E		
B	O	L	E	S		I	T	S		P	O	S	I	T
		C	E	L	L	O		M	O	T	E	T	S	
U	N	R	E	E	L		P	O	L					
H	A	U	L		A	N	T	E	P	E	N	U	L	T
H	I	L	L		M	O	O	N		M	A	N	I	A
U	V	E	A		A	G	R	A		I	V	I	E	D
H	E	R	R		S	O	I	L		C	E	T	U	S

PUZZLE 30

R	E	D	S		B	A	D	G	E		T	B	A	R
O	P	A	H		R	U	I	N	S		H	O	P	E
M	I	D	I		A	R	E	A	S		R	O	E	S
	C	O	N	Q	U	I	S	T	A	D	O	R	S	
			L	U	N	G		Y	O	N				
M	E	D	E	A		A	B	A		T	E	E	T	H
U	N	E	A	S	E		O	D	E		V	I	A	
S	E	L	F	I	M	P	R	O	V	E	M	E	N	T
I	M	F		U	R	N		E	V	I	N	C	E	
C	A	T	C	H		Y	E	T		E	A	S	T	S
			H	E	S		H	E	R	O				
	I	D	E	N	T	I	C	A	L	T	W	I	N	
A	C	H	E		E	L	E	M	I		I	D	E	A
B	O	A	R		A	I	R	E	D		N	O	R	M
O	N	L	Y		M	A	N	S	E		G	L	O	P

PUZZLE 31

T	A	L	C		E	P	I	C		C	W	T
A	R	E	A		P	I	N	O	T		V	A	R	Y
M	I	S	D	I	R	E	C	T	S		E	M	I	R
E	A	T		R	I	C	H		H	E	R	E	T	O
			M	I	N	E		A	I	R	Y			
D	E	T	E	S	T		G	U	R	G	L	I	N	G
O	M	E	N		C	U	R	T		I	D	E	A	
L	I	S	T		A	R	I	A	S		G	I	R	L
O	L	L	A		V	I	L	E		H	O	V	E	
R	E	A	L	T	I	M	E		F	A	T	T	E	N
			N	E	A	P		D	A	G	S			
T	H	R	O	A	T		T	R	I	O		S	A	E
R	O	U	T		O	C	E	A	N	G	O	I	N	G
I	S	L	E		R	E	A	C	T		A	N	T	I
G	E	E		P	R	O	S		F	E	E	S		

PUZZLE 32

B	A	Y		S	H	A	D		S	T	O	A	T
E	N	E		C	E	L	E	B		C	H	I	L	I
N	E	O		A	R	E	N	A		R	E	L	I	C
I	M	M	U	N	E	S	Y	S	T	E	M			
G	I	A	N	T		R	U	E		C	H	I		
N	A	N	S		A	S	S	A	I		T	H	U	D
		C	A	N	O	N		T	O	R	I	E	S	
	P	A	R	T	Y	P	O	L	I	T	I	C	S	
B	E	S	E	E	M		R	I	O	T	S			
A	N	E	W		O	F	T	E	N		E	R	S	T
D	N	A		I	R	E			A	C	U	T	E	
		P	R	E	D	I	G	E	S	T	I	O	N	
M	E	D	I	A		U	S	E	R	S		N	O	D
A	S	Y	E	T		P	I	N	N	A		E	G	O
S	T	E	R	E		S	T	E	M		D	E	N	

111

PUZZLE 33

C	F	C		A	J	A	R		K	N	I	T		
K	I	L	O		R	U	N	E		O	I	L	E	R
I	R	I	S		E	M	I	T		R	H	I	N	O
E	R	E		M	A	P		D	I	E		A	T	E
V	I	R	T	U			R	A	W					
		E	G	O		B	E	E		E	D	D	A	
V	E	D	A		F	L	A	G			B	E	E	B
E	R	A		T	O	N	G	A		A	L	E		
R	I	N	G		G	A	S	P		E	D	I	T	
B	E	A	U		S	O	L		E	L	K			
		Y	O	U			A	E	R	I	E			
B	R	O		L	E	I		M	O	W		E	M	U
O	I	L	E	D		S	N	A	P		S	T	A	R
A	L	I	B	I		L	I	N	E		E	R	G	O
	L	O	B	E		E	L	A	N		W	O	O	

PUZZLE 34

_	M	R	S			B	L	T		O	P	A	H	
C	I	A	O		O	L	I	O		C	E	C	U	M
H	A	N	D	C	L	A	S	P		T	R	A	L	A
A	U	G		L	I	M	P	I	D		P	A	R	
P	L	Y		A	V	E	S		N	E	A	P		
		O	N	E			E	A	G	L	E	T		
A	M	I	R		S	A	N	G		G	E	L	I	D
B	A	L	M		L	E	I		P	L	E	A		
A	G	L	O	W		P	E	S	O		H	A	R	M
	I	N	L	A	W	S		P	U	S				
E	U	R	O		S	T	E	P		I	N	S		
E	M	S		K	I	M	O	N	O		D	U	O	
N	A	S	A	L		N	O	N	E	N	T	I	T	Y
E	D	E	M	A		S	T	A	R		I	O	T	A
	E	S	P	Y		T	E	L		S	T	Y		

PUZZLE 35

S	H	A	G		O	S	L	O			L	U	R	E	D
P	E	R	U		I	C	E	D		A	N	O	D	E	
A	R	I	L		L	O	G	O		T	I	T	A	N	
C	O	L	L	E	C	T	O	R	S	I	T	E	M	S	
E	N	S		V	A	T			A	N	Y				
		G	I	N		O	N	T	O		L	S	D		
F	R	A	N	C		A	W	A	Y		K	I	T	E	
R	E	L	A	T	I	V	E	P	R	O	N	O	U	N	
E	A	S	T		D	I	N	E		P	E	N	N	Y	
E	D	O		A	I	D	S		G	E	E				
		P	R	O		B	U	R		P	U	S			
A	N	T	I	I	M	P	E	R	I	A	L	I	S	T	
G	O	I	N	G		E	V	I	L		A	Q	U	A	
E	A	R	T	H		R	E	N	T		P	U	R	R	
S	H	O	O	T		I	N	K	Y		P	E	P	S	

PUZZLE 36

M	A	C	A	W		E	L	B	E		R	O	S	A
O	V	O	L	O		R	O	A	M		O	V	E	R
C	O	S	M	E	T	I	C	S	U	R	G	E	R	Y
H	I	T	S		A	C	H	E		A	U	R	A	L
A	D	S		B	R	A	N		O	G	E	E		
		T	A	N		E	A	T	S		A	T	M	
S	U	G	A	R		P	S	S	T		S	T	O	A
T	R	O	U	B	L	E	S	H	O	O	T	E	R	S
I	S	N	T		A	R	M	Y		M	U	N	C	H
R	A	D		T	R	I	O		P	E	N			
		O	C	A	S		N	E	O	N		A	P	R
A	T	L	A	S		T	S	A	R		E	S	A	U
Q	U	I	C	K	W	I	T	T	E	D	N	E	S	S
U	R	E	A		O	R	E	O		A	V	A	S	T
A	F	R	O		T	E	R	N		D	Y	N	E	S

112

PUZZLE 37

P	T	A		T	B	A	R		R	O	S	A
P	A	W	N		Y	O	K	E		U	N	I	F	Y
E	P	I	C		P	L	A	T		M	E	T	R	O
P	U	L		J	O	T		E	B	B		E	O	N
S	A	L	S	A			O	A	T			
	T	W	O		C	I	A		H	O	O	T
S	H	A	Y		T	S	A	R		E	N	V	Y
H	A	G		T	H	R	O	B		C	E	P
A	L	E	S		M	E	N	U		G	E	N	E
D	O	D	O		R	O	T		Y	E	N	
	P	E	A			N	U	R	S	E
A	A	H		R	Y	E		C	U	D		H	A	W
S	N	A	F	U		A	E	O	N		B	Y	T	E
H	E	T	U	P		S	L	E	D		E	M	I	R
W	E	N	T		E	D	D	O		T	E	N

PUZZLE 38

P	A	L		W	A	D		E	R	A	S
E	A	S	E		S	E	G	O		M	U	F	T	I
D	U	C	K	B	I	L	L	S		U	G	L	I	S
I	L	O		R	E	S	E	T	S		A	R	M
T	I	T		A	S	H	Y		P	I	T	T
	M	E	T		R	A	M	R	O	D
E	D	G	E		A	S	E	A		P	I	X	I	E
R	E	A	D		L	E	I		B	I	E	R
R	A	T	I	O		I	N	L	Y		A	N	T	E
R	E	C	A	S	T		E	E	L
	H	I	F	I		O	R	A	L		K	I	T
B	R	O		R	E	C	E	S	S		O	D	E
R	O	U	G	H		G	U	A	T	E	M	A	L	A
A	S	S	A	I		A	L	L	Y		A	L	E	S
Y	E	L	P		D	I	M		T	A	R

PUZZLE 39

F	E	D	S		P	S	S	T		G	L	I	T	Z
O	K	R	A		O	P	A	H		R	I	S	H	I
L	I	A	R		S	A	L	E		A	T	M	A	N
I	N	C	I	D	E	N	T	A	L	M	U	S	I	C
A	G	O		A	U	K		I	M	P
	E	R	R		C	A	G	E		G	M	T
O	R	A	T	E		A	R	C	H		A	R	E	A
D	E	P	A	R	T	M	E	N	T	S	T	O	R	E
O	D	E	S		H	O	S	E		H	O	T	E	L
R	O	D		D	A	K	S		M	A	M
	C	O	N		E	A	R		A	S	S
S	H	R	I	N	K	I	N	G	V	I	O	L	E	T
T	I	A	R	A		M	A	G	I		U	P	T	O
E	V	I	C	T		A	V	O	N		C	H	I	C
M	E	L	E	E		M	E	N	S		H	A	N	K

PUZZLE 40

F	C	C		A	F	R	O		K	I	L	O
S	E	A	R		S	L	U	R		I	M	A	G	O
P	I	N	T		T	E	N	T		O	P	T	E	D
A	G	O		S	I	X		S	A	W		H	E	D
S	N	E	A	K		L	A	Y		
	R	I	G		P	I	P		O	G	L	E
M	O	O	T		Y	A	R	N		N	O	U	N
A	I	D		P	R	O	N	G		I	T	D
K	N	O	W		M	E	S	A		O	N	E	S
O	K	R	A		I	S	M		P	A	D
	S	I	R			Y	E	M	E	N
A	P	P		N	E	W		L	I	E		A	N	A
S	O	U	L	S		A	C	I	D		K	I	E	V
P	U	R	E	E		N	O	N	E		E	L	M	Y
F	L	A	T		T	O	G	A		G	S	A

PUZZLE 41

N	O	G		S	C	A	G		F	L	A	W
H	O	M	E		U	R	D	U		L	A	N	E	S
O	V	E	N		P	A	I	R		U	B	O	A	T
W	A	G	E	S		Y	O	U	R		O	N	L	Y
L	E	A		T	W	O	S		O	E	R
		R	U	I	N		H	A	M		L	E	O
B	R	A	N	D	T		M	E	N	U		O	D	D
I	O	T	A		E	O	N		E	R	G	O
E	D	O		P	A	L	M		B	O	R	D	E	R
R	E	M		I	R	K		T	A	N	G
	V	E	T		A	S	H	Y		E	G	G
L	A	M	E		Y	E	A	H		X	E	N	O	N
S	T	A	N	K		D	R	I	B		R	A	G	A
D	O	G	I	E		D	O	R	Y		S	T	O	W
	P	I	N	G		A	N	T	E		E	E	L

PUZZLE 42

	W	A	S		M	B	A		T	A	L	C
B	A	L	K		D	E	L	I		I	N	A	L	L
U	N	B	I	G	O	T	E	D		S	T	R	A	Y
G	N	U		E	G	R	E	S	S		R	Y	E
S	A	M		A	T	O	P		K	E	P	I
		B	R	A		B	A	T	I	K	S
I	N	C	A		G	I	B	E		A	L	I	E	N
D	I	O	R		T	A	R		O	N	T	O
S	P	U	T	A		E	R	G	O		T	S	A	R
	A	N	O	N	Y	M		P	U	S
	S	K	Y	E		T	H	E	N		L	E	T
S	E	E		T	Y	R	A	N	T		A	D	O
E	U	L	E	R		M	A	I	L	O	R	D	E	R
W	R	O	T	E		C	I	T	Y		A	L	M	S
O	R	C	S		A	N	I		T	E	A

PUZZLE 43

	S	T	Y		C	A	R	E		S	A	I	D
S	L	O	E		O	P	U	S		C	D	R	O	M
A	U	N	T		D	E	E	P		O	Z	O	N	E
K	E	G		L	A	X		Y	A	P		N	E	T
I	S	S	U	E			S	E	W
		S	A	C		F	O	P		O	A	F	S
M	A	M	A		A	J	A	R		E	X	I	T
A	G	E		M	A	C	A	W		E	R	A
R	U	M	P		D	E	L	I		E	L	M	Y
L	E	E	R		S	E	T		G	E	M
		Y	O	U			E	U	R	O	S
A	C	E		A	N	D		G	E	L		A	I	M
L	O	V	E	S		D	I	A	L		T	I	L	E
A	L	I	B	I		A	R	E	S		S	T	E	W
	A	L	B	S		Y	A	L	E		P	A	D

PUZZLE 44

	R	A	F		A	L	B		O	V	U	M
H	U	L	A		B	O	O	T		C	E	R	I	A
A	N	O	N		O	G	L	E		A	T	A	L	L
T	O	N	G	A		J	U	M	P		C	L	O	P
E	N	E		B	I	A	S		A	A	H
		G	L	O	M		M	R	S		H	O	P
B	O	L	E	Y	N		O	U	R	S		I	C	Y
R	A	I	L		A	D	D		A	F	A	R
O	T	T		L	A	N	D		V	A	L	I	S	E
S	H	E		E	N	D		P	A	P	A
		D	U	E		O	A	T	S		F	C	C
I	N	D	O		W	A	R	M		E	N	J	O	Y
C	O	A	T	I		N	I	P	A		O	O	H	S
E	N	T	E	R		T	E	A	L		G	R	O	T
E	A	S	E		E	L	S	E		O	D	E

PUZZLE 45

PUZZLE 46

PUZZLE 47

PUZZLE 48

PUZZLE 49

E	R	R	A	T	A		A	S	H		M	A	T	E
R	E	U	B	E	N		U	K	E		A	I	R	Y
A	S	S	O	C	I	A	T	E	D	E	G	R	E	E
S	T	E	M			S	O	L		R	I	S	E	R
			B	O	A	T		E	N	E				
S	P	A		A	R	I	S	T	O	C	R	A	C	Y
C	A	V	O	R	T		T	O	R	T	I	L	L	A
A	S	I	A		P	A	N		F	L	O	C		
R	E	S	T	S	T	O	P		O	A	F	I	S	H
P	O	O	H	P	O	O	H	I	N	G		S	E	T
			O	W	L		B	O	O	M				
T	A	B	O	O		S	K	I		E	T	U	I	
S	M	A	L	L	M	I	N	D	E	D	N	E	S	S
A	M	I	D		I	D	O		M	O	S	L	E	M
R	O	T	S		D	E	W		S	C	A	L	D	S

PUZZLE 50

	F	B	I		B	Y	T	E		R	A	N	D	
E	A	R	S		L	A	I	R		A	L	O	U	D
G	U	A	M		U	R	N	S		B	E	R	N	E
I	N	K		R	E	D		E	B	B		M	E	N
S	A	Y	S	O				O	I	L				
		L	E	I		C	H	A		O	G	R	E	
O	N	L	Y		T	A	L	A		X	R	A	Y	
F	I	E		S	C	A	L	A		O	R	E		
F	L	E	W		H	I	F	I		A	G	E	S	
S	E	R	A		G	Y	M		L	O	B			
		D	U	O				D	A	T	E	D		
A	P	E		S	T	Y		C	A	D		H	A	Y
L	O	U	G	H		A	W	L	S		D	O	V	E
B	O	R	N	E		N	E	A	T		I	R	E	S
H	O	U	R		K	I	W	I		E	N	S		

Congratulations

You Finished!!!

MORE BOOKS BY JOURNALS INK

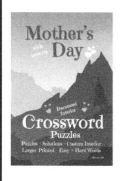   

CROSSWORD WORD SEARCH MAZE SUDOKU

facebook.com/JournalsInk
pinterest.com/journalsink

Made in the USA
Las Vegas, NV
08 December 2021